Ladies and Gentlemen

Ladies and Gentlemen

A PARCEL OF RECONSIDERATIONS

By

BRANCH CABELL

"These, being dead, have been made the forgers of many lies, now that their memorable doings are proverbs of dust, and their defences are defences of clay."

Wildside Press: 2003

Published by
Wildside Press, LLC
P.O. Box 301
Holicong, PA 18928-0301 USA
www.wildsidepress.com

Wildside Press Edition: MMIII

My Dear Richard Butler Glaenzer:

Your letters, it occurs to me, have been of unfailing interest ever since I first read that first letter, in the New York *Times* of 24 December, 1904, which besought its readers to cease writing to that periodical any further nonsense, either in praise or blame, of a then recent novel, *The Eagle's Shadow*. It would be a great deal more sensible, you pointed out, to rejoice that the terrors of Christmas shopping were for the while ended than to waste any more paper on young Cabell's ephemeralities.

Well, the whirligig of Time has so far brought in his revenges that your present vocation forbids you to discourage—with quite such frankness, at least—any reasonable publicity for my books. Instead, it has now for some while been your doom to read, to edit, and to advertise them. Nor can I estimate how many, as one should say, yet other critical, but all-friendly, letters I have read over your signature during the thirty years of our acquaintance.

I infer (through, it may be, no hard and fast rule of logic) that this book of letters, to which you have contributed a large quota of inspiring suggestions, ought to be thus dedicated, in token of its author's debt, and forgiveness, and friendship.

Ophelia, Virginia   *Branch Cabell*
June, 1934

BIBLIOGRAPHICAL

Excepting only the epistle to Ananias (which figured in the first issue of *Direction*) no letter in this collection of letters has been issued until to-day in its complete form. One remarks, though, for the general benefit of the bibliophile, that in the *American Spectator* have appeared abridgements of the Prologue and of the fifth, the sixth, the twelfth, the thirteenth, the sixteenth, and the nineteenth letter. Much of the twentieth letter was used as an introduction to the Modern Library edition of *Jurgen*: and some half-dozen paragraphs from the fourteenth letter and four paragraphs from the seventeenth letter have been printed in, respectively, the *Saturday Review of Literature* and the *Nation*. Of the remaining eleven letters, and of the acrostic Palinode—if indeed the precise claims of accuracy need venture thus far in the obvious—no part hitherto has been published.

CONTENTS

Contents

Ladies and Gentlemen

PROLOGUE:

Which Treats of Writing without Tears

*"The thrice three Muses mourning for the death
Of 'Letters,' late deceased in beggary."*

PROLOGUE:

Which Treats of Writing without Tears

It was flattering of you, Sir, to ask that I explain, to the readers of the magazine which you ably edit, my personal ideas as to "the position of the American literary artist in this time of unrest and indecision." I was suitably grateful. I regarded with every appropriate sentiment the opportunity thus offered me to unloose the full force of my wrath, anguish, indignation, and rhetoric, as to the dilemma of those high-minded beings who (as you have nicely expressed it) "write without a pedlar's sordid regard for pragmatic values," in a republic so unappreciative of its literary martyrs that—still to employ your phrasing, Sir—"their very existence is sometimes begrudged."

Ladies and Gentlemen

I replied therefore by return of post. And after typing out my heartbroken regrets for my inability to join in the symposium which your magazine is conducting, I began sorrowfully to reflect that this sort of nonsense is quite probably immortal.

In any case, all this public self-pitying, by our less widely read writers, is but formally allied with facts. I think it, for example, a not irrelevant fact that the persons who are most volubly bothered by the lot of the literary artist in America happen not to be literary artists. And in saying this, I intend, I assure you, no reproach. To the contrary, so often as I hear these lamenters—"when in a wailful choir," as Keats puts it, "the small gnats sing,"—then I reflect, with the most kindly sort of sympathy, that for some years these men have been doing their very utmost to become literary artists. I mean only that, in reading such bewailments of America's literary tastes, one notices, almost always, that the fate of the elegist, as a writer, would have been equally unconducive to optimism in any other country, merely because he was created with no talent for writing. It seems unfair: but at this late date, what is anybody to do about it? I mean, in

6

brief, that you will not find any writer whom a respectable quorum of judges might rank as important, or even as a fairly competent craftsman, bewailing the lot of the literary artist in America.

Here, I admit, enters the complication that some of our now elderly and best authors (as our modest best averages) have during the not distant past made considerable money by their writing. It was an indiscretion which laid them open to being rebuked, by less fortunate persons, as degraded slaves and foul panders to the capitalist system. Such parasites, their indignant rivals might well remark, were in any discussion of æsthetics *hors concours*. (Human nature being what it is, the actual remark was a great deal more uncivil.) To-day, however, when indigence has become epidemic, under the able guidance of Colonel Roosevelt's best-known cousin, this reproach is far out-of-date. To-day these cashiered hirelings, like everybody else, are earning very little money, now that the strange old American custom of buying books has perished—and still, it is to be noted, the obstinate creatures keep silent as to the sad lot of the artist in America. That is because, my dear Sir, they happen actually to be artists, whom their art contents in its own special, illogical, and high fashion, and upon whom an innate form of insanity acts as a cordial.

*

*   *

For my part, in looking backward, I can but wonder at this perennial pother. Nothing, it seems to me, interferes with the American writer except his own frailty. I at least have been writing now for the third part of a century. Throughout this while I have been permitted to write exactly what I wanted to write, and to publish as much of it as I desired. I have not (I pause to observe, in mere self-defence) made any ponderable money out of authorship: and for my publishers' sake I regret this. Personally, I do not see upon what grounds I should be paid for having diverted myself throughout thirty-three years hand-running.

I continue to look back. I remember that what I have published in magazine form during the last thirty-three years has now and then suffered from a little genteel editing—in which, even at its silliest,

8

Of Writing without Tears

the humor atoned for the prudery. I recall, for example, how that great editor of *Harper's Magazine*, Henry M. Alden (with I prefer not to imagine what shakings of his grand gray head) struck out from my text a "belly" in favor of a "paunch." I recall too how my esteemed mentor, Henry S. Canby—in editing that very weekly paper which is still issued, upon unexplained grounds, as the *Saturday Review of Literature*—wrote in "life" where I had horrifically, but at least rationally, typed "semen."

Moreover do I recollect how yet another well-known Henry blushingly made complete nonsense out of one of my paragraphs by putting, at first "love," and then "sex," in place of "coition." But, almost always, this editing took the shape of excisions such as, in a great many cases, even I could see were improvements. And in any event I was left free to remedy every bit of this editing when the essay or the short story came to its final estate in book form, so that no large, no permanent, hurt was done.

Just once, I can recall also, I have found pressed against one of my books (because it appeared to speak lightly of papal infallibility) a quite frankly trumped-up charge of lewdness. Even at the time, the illogic of this seemed amusing. The upshot, at all events, was a collapse of the pious fraud, in due course, with no more harmful results than to advertise this particular book at the expense of its fellows, and handsomely to increase its sales.

Well, then, my dear Sir, with these negligible exceptions, nobody has ever tried in any degree to interfere with or to check, or to color, my writing whatsoever I elected to write during thirty-three years. Throughout that period I have enjoyed a free hand, a quota of applause, and a gratifying belittlement by the more literal-minded. It follows that (despite some large native talents for exaggerating any personal mishap) I am not able to feel martyrized by my American birth or by my dependency on an American audience. So far as goes my personal experience, the American writer, during the last thirty-three years, has been permitted, and to a certain extent encouraged, to do the very best of which he was capable. And if—just now and then— that best happened, after all, not to be in every one of its features an earth-staggering masterpiece, this outcome may well have been (I suggest diffidently) not so much the fault of America's cultural crassness

Of Writing without Tears

as of its writer's failure to start life as a genius of the first order. Occasionally babies forget to do that.

*

*　　　*

For the rest, I incline here to resent the far too common assumption that the artist in letters has, in some way, a semi-divine right to expect from his art a living wage. That notion really is a bit too irrational to be cherished even by *Homo sapiens,* because all experience contradicts it. All literary history shows that the beginning author has entered his name in a lottery in which the haphazardly awarded prizes are few and not huge. In every known civilization the literary artist has at times earned a moderate living, as with Thackeray and Shakespeare and Virgil, and at other times has earned virtually nothing, as with Gissing and Villon and Ovid. In America the case is not otherwise: nor do I know, upon the whole, of any reason why the case ought to be otherwise.

"Literature is a fine staff, but a poor crutch," runs the old saying. I think this a profound saying:

for from every standpoint of morality, as well as from the natural standpoint of his dependants, it is wicked for a writer to depend solely upon his art for his alimony. Indeed, toward his art also his first duty is to inherit, rather early in life, a large income, so that he may always write only that which he desires to write, for his own diversion. Very often have I deplored my own neglect of this duty. For I take it that a writer who has ignored this plain obligation must expect to see both his art and himself suffer. When once he has put his muse to work to support him, then he becomes in some sort a pimp; and he is but too apt to develop a melting eye for "pragmatic values." He observes, perhaps, the more liberally paying magazines with new charity; or he turns, it may be, from regarding his own indigent household with the emotions becoming in a fond father and a tender husband, to regarding Hollywood with envy.

Nevertheless, my dear Sir, in no symposium as to the sad lot of the artist in America will any truth-loving writer who has attained middle-life elect to shed typographic tears. He knows that, to the contrary, in America his lot has for a great while been enviable. Year in, year out, he has done precisely

12

that which he wanted to do, the despair and the reprehension of the thrifty. To-day all those of his most thrifty advisers who are neither in prison nor, as yet, out on bail, are in bankruptcy. But the confirmed writer (to whom bankruptcy can reveal, at worst, only the trite features of a long familiar neighbor) is whistling in his writing room, now that he sets to work on his some-and-twentieth book. And he finds that, for some reason or another reason, his thoughts take, yet again, an epistolary turn.

❋

❋   ❋

It was Charles Lamb, you will remember, who bid his age go hang, and declared he would henceforward write for antiquity. Hereinafter I have so far carried out this resolve that each of the included letters is addressed to this or the other person nowadays so long dead as to make virtually certain the outcome that no one of these letters will ever be answered. To this extent, Sir, I may assert that I also have disregarded "pragmatic values."

Ladies and Gentlemen

Nor need anyone inquire, I trust, for what reason it is to this or the other ossuary that I address myself. To begin with, the grounds for my own personal interest have been made obvious in sundry cases, even at the risk of egotism. But in the main, I have written these letters because each of the deceased persons addressed hereinafter appears to me to have been misunderstood somewhat noteworthily.

We think about Penelope, for example, as a heroine of romance: which is quite as though we were to think about Esther Waters—or, perhaps a more exact instance, about Mrs. George F. Babbitt —as a heroine of romance. We think about Tutankhamen almost as if we were thinking about a definite person: which is a delusion. We think about Jonah, the son of Amittai, as a synonym for misfortune: which fact itself is both a misfortune and an insanity. And we think about Geoffrey Rudel as being the protagonist of that tragedy wherein occurred his death: which is but to assume that either Banquo or Duncan may very well be the protagonist of *Macbeth*. So is it, in short, with all the persons whom I address here. Each one of them has acquired in some degree an unmerited reputation which remains flatly at odds with—or which stays at any rate irrelevant to—the known facts of his or of her life.

Let not any rattlepate misunderstand me! Mine is not the reformer's mania. I would for no half instant challenge any one of these samples of what Sir Thomas Browne has described—in his fine mouth-filling phrase—as *pseudodoxia epidemica.* The task, to begin with, is hopeless: moreover, all these victims and beneficiaries of misrepresentation are nowadays a long way past caring about that which we may or may not say concerning them: and besides that, the injustice—it is an odd thing—has in each case been of some partial benefit to mankind at large.

It follows that, to my finding, the upshot in each case has been gratifying enough. And it follows also that—if but "as one that loves his fellow men," to the limited extent permitted by reason—the considerate person will be led heartily to applaud the triumph of each salutary bit of injustice hereinafter recorded.

THE FIRST LETTER:

To Penelope, the Daughter of
Icarius

"Daughter of Icarius, wise Penelope, take courage, and let not thy heart be careful for these things."

THE FIRST LETTER:

To Penelope, the Daughter of Icarius

With what praises, revered wife of Odysseus, may one approach you fittingly? Through the bright cool morning of Homer's world you move statelily, the first and loveliest of all Stoics, the most perfect and pious and wise, and, by long odds, the most rightfully self-complacent of antiquity's women. Yours was not the divine beauty of Calypso, nor the bedrugging witch-wiles of Circe, nor even the engaging innocence of Nausicaa: and yet, to shrewd Odysseus, were you more dear than any of these, and the most desirable of all earth's inhabitants. A quaint outcome it seems, that, although the *Odyssey* has been regarded from countless standpoints, the tale has not yet been appraised as being what it actually is—as the history of a man's strong and all-surmounting love for his own wife, and as a large parable of the average, because successful, marriage.

A many witlings, in the world's stormy evening, Lady, have come—I know not how—to assume that, because marriage has outlasted the centuries, it must nowadays be an obsolete and admittedly unsatisfying custom. By such prattlers a contented marriage is suspect. They encounter it everywhere; and yet always to them it smacks of hypocrisy. At utmost may they shruggingly pardon its practitioners, as mid-Victorian. These sciolists find it not possible to associate any humbug so parochial with Homer's heroic and untrammeled world. Nevertheless has this Homer written a not wholly negligible epic, in twenty-four books, of which the protagonist is no man and no woman, but marriage itself—that mere, that unromantic, and (what enviably young wise-acres find to be indescribably more shocking) that contented monogamy by the staid and staunch magic of which you, renowned Queen, and your much-travelled husband were held ensorcelled.

It is not easy to imagine any words more prosaic or more commonplace or, in brief, more bourgeois

To Penelope

than, "Well, but I must be getting home to my wife." Yet is this the continued refrain, and, as it were, the mainspring, of the world's supreme romantic masterpiece in the way of epic poetry.

It is true that your historian, this Homer, has written an *Iliad*, about the doings of your relatives in the siege of Troy. Men praise it highly. None the less do I believe that mankind's so loudly expressed preference for the *Iliad* as the more admirable of this Homer's epics has always been somewhat a matter of tradition and an act of faith rather than of reason. The story of the *Iliad*, it seems to me, is not well contrived: it ends inconclusively; and if the poet has indeed been telling us about *menin Achilleos*, he has wandered meanwhile into a surprising number of bypaths which reveal no plain connection with either Achilles or his wrath. How different is the well-nigh perfect and arrowy-swift construction of the *Odyssey*, wherein all deals, in one way or another, with your husband's overmastering need to return to you!

Moreover, to our modern taste, the Greek leaders who occupy the foreground of the *Iliad* are a somewhat unbearable set of fools and rogues and bullies. To you, Lady, this can hardly come as news, since each one of them was, in one degree or another, your cousin whom you regarded with the cruelly clear and unsparing gaze of close kinship. Well! I would not uphold your husband Odysseus as a model gentleman in his every action: but he does retain a reader's sympathy throughout the story of his return to you, whereas Achilles nauseates any mature-minded person a good while before the *Iliad* can be read through.

*

*   *

With literary questions, however, it appears probable you do not much concern yourself in the Isles of Bliss. I imagine you did not greatly care for poetry. Here we lack any conclusive evidence. You are shown in contact with but one bard, with Phemius, and him you requested to desist from poetizing; but it was upon emotional rather than æsthetic grounds. None the less am I sure that you during your mortal life would never have found the time for an epic in twenty-four books; nor do I think that you, being immortal, have yet put aside

To Penelope

your household duties long enough to read through the *Odyssey* . . . For one knows, somehow, that in the Isles of Bliss you are still about your housekeeping: otherwise to you were the place not blissful. With you, your home came first; and Odysseus, howsoever sincerely lamented might be his absence, was not quite so important as the maintenance of your thrifty and comfortable housekeeping.

To this fact you yourself certified. When it seemed that, at long last, you in self-defence must now marry one or another of the Suitors, you did not cry out for Odysseus. You deplored instead the harsh need of leaving your home, which was so fair and well filled with the small comforts, the modern conveniences, and to a rational degree with the luxuries also, of life. You protested you would forever remember in your dreams, not the husband of your youth, Lady, but the beloved house over which you had ruled throughout some-and-twenty years. It seems an odd *cri du cœur*; and yet across the centuries it rings true to any man—of, as they say, a certain age—who has been so fortunate as to marry a really first-class housekeeper.

So we praise you not for your tenderness, renowned Queen, but because in all your doings you were sedate and acute and stout-hearted. For ten years the mob of Suitors wooed you in your supposed widowhood, devouring your well-tended cattle and sheep, and swigging down your kegs of good homemade wine. No less strenuously than Troy were you besieged, for the same while: but unlike Troy, you were not ever taken. Implacably and smilingly you fobbed off the ruinous mob of your besetters, throughout ten years, with your never-failing excuses, and with your pious delays, and—there is not any other term, Lady—with your outright lies. For decorum forbid, you said, that you should take a second husband before you had woven a shroud for your present father-in-law. So you labored publicly upon this polite tribute to Laertes day after day, and at night you unravelled it privately, thus making of "the web of Penelope" a useful synonym for work never completed.

Meanwhile, in your quiet and matter-of-fact fashion, you at reasonable intervals would suggest that, by every rule of good breeding, it was customary for a lover to approach the wooed lady with suitable gifts. In this way did you obtain from the Suitors—from Antinous and Eurymachus and Peisander and Eurydamas and all the others—an

To Penelope

infinity of embroidered robes and gold chains and brooches and earrings and necklaces. One infers that, so long as they insisted upon infesting your palace, and upon obtaining from you, in default of a privilege more tender, three meals a day, it seemed to you only right they should pay board. It is the economy of Mrs. Todgers, far from exalted; but one delights in you, nevertheless, for having practised this economy thus shrewdly, in, of all places, an epic poem, and, in of all rôles, as the heroine of an epic.

In brief, the heroine of the world's most great romantic poem has in her nature no least tinge of romance or of poetry. The goal toward which Odysseus strove, across the tumbling and hungry seas of his wonderland, was a well-equipped home presided over by a tactful and competent, if a somewhat narrow-minded, housewife. The world displayed to him one by one its treasures; fair Circe beckoned, the clear-voiced Sirens sang languorously, and in a wood of alder and poplar and sweet-smelling cypress-trees, divine Calypso proffered him immortality. Hell loosed its terrors before him, and at his heels was angry Poseidon, the dark-tressed earth-shaker, an infuriate supreme god, bent upon the destruction of Odysseus. He viewed these matters warily, with experienced, half-amused eyes. He shrugged then, saying, "Well, but I must be getting home to my wife."

We know, Penelope, that he succeeded in his endeavor. It is an old and heart-stirring tale, how your palace was rid of those pestering Suitors, "so that their bodies lay heaped the one upon another, like fishes that the fishermen have drawn up from out of the gray sea in a net"; and how Odysseus found you still to be fair and faithful and stainless, after the twenty years of severance. We know that he won back, at thus great adventure, to you, the all-perfect wife, whom his deep heart desired steadfastly. Yes; it is in its every feature a most satisfactory love story, in so far as Odysseus was concerned.

*

*   *

And you, renowned Queen? One perceives that you were unfeignedly glad to see Odysseus back again, in his proper place. You gave way to no large ardors: that was not your fashion. To the contrary,

To Penelope

it was Odysseus who "wept as he embraced his beloved and true wife." You remained coolly affec-
tionate. And you checked any further *redigratio
amoris* until your long-lost husband had explained
to you more amply just what Teiresias had pro-
phesied as to the immediate future. That was a
matter, you felt, of some real importance: once it
was settled, you ascended the bedstead of brightly
inlaid olive-wood willingly enough, if without any
special enthusiasm.

There Homer, with a gentlemanly reserve, leaves
you, in bed with your husband, affording him docilely "his fill of love as of old." But we well know
that thereafter you just as tactfully looked out for
the comfort of Odysseus in all other respects. You
did not ask, I am sure, any awkward questions about
Calypso or Circe or the Sirens, or any other of those
minxes whom your husband met during the ten
years of his return homeward. You, with your cool
good sense, knew very well what such creatures must
amount to, eventually, in any sensible man's life—
and what, too, the most sensible man must amount
to before their immoral seductions. So you accepted
these goings-on perforce, with a little mild con-
tempt, but without spitefully prying into them.

27

Goodness only knew what the man had been up to; and it was not as if any rational wife could expect him of all persons to tell you the truth about it. Odysseus was back again, that was the main point: a husband's place is the home.

And with you, the second point was to make his home comfortable for this headstrong and shifty male (so long as he did not interfere with your home's proper management) for the rest of your allotted time, all day and every day, until you had grown too feeble to pamper him. Thus truly was Odysseus thrice-blessed, renowned Queen, in having a wife who left, for a man of his age, nothing to be desired. Nor did it much trouble him that the true "web of Penelope" had its arachnean aspect.

*

*   *

Well, and so is it with many of us, Lady, we blundering male creatures who have attained to gray hairs and to some stinted portion of judgment. In youth, like your Odysseus, we have wooed the golden Helen, whom every lad must adore in the

To Penelope

perturbed April season of his living, and whom no man wins, and whom graybeards forget gradually. We have had our delight in battle, our defeats, and our little victories here and there. We have escaped, somehow, the continuous maraudings of time and disease and dishonor and poverty—the Scyllas and the Cyclôpes and the Læstrygonians and the Charybdises of our haphazard travelling—where our less fortunate comrades did not survive these perils. Behind each one of us is a Circe, a few Sirens, and a fond Calypso or two,—whose wiles we evaded, or whose love we relinquished, for this or the other reason. Behind us is much passion and wonderment, and, in brief, our youth is behind us, with all the splendid, toplofty and irrational magnanimities of youth. We have journeyed a long way. We are a bit travel-stained, not merely in body. But those of us who were most lucky have won, in the undeserved outcome, to our little Ithaca and to our special Penelope.

She is not of all women the most beautiful or the most amorous or the most brilliant, it may be: but she has her own deep wisdom, denied to golden Helen and unguessed at by any wanton Sirens, that wisdom through which Penelope creates and rules

29

over the quiet afternoon of each lucky man's living. Yes, and like Circe, Penelope puts forth a transforming magic, making of us not rude untidy swine, but performing a miracle far more great. Affably, gently, and implacably, she converts the egotistic and self-reliant hero into the sedately contented husband.

THE SECOND LETTER:

To Tutankhamen, Lord of the Two Lands

"He hath conquered this land without opposition to his advance, the King of the South and the North, the son of Ra, beloved of Amen of Napt."

THE SECOND LETTER:

To Tutankhamen, Lord of the Two Lands

From your long repose, throughout the length of some thirty-three centuries, in the most holy Valley of Kings, they brought you forth into a famousness such as no other Pharaoh has achieved. Strong warriors and wise law-givers, great builders and priests and poets and many shrewd statesmen, had ruled over your Egypt, by the scores and by the hundreds, each earning assiduously a world-wide glory; basking in it for his season; and departing thence into the obscurity of a footnote. To you alone of the Pharaohs was it granted to become "news," the more striking because of its well-nigh incredible antiquity. From the Valley of Kings, in brief, you passed suddenly into the rotogravure sections.

33

Ladies and Gentlemen

We beheld then all the superb gear which you had laid away against your needs in the Fields of Ialu. Here were your thrones and your war chariots, overlaid with sheet gold and adorned with inlaid stone and faience; your beds of carved ebony-wood and ivory, inset richly with gems, and so shaped as to represent lions or cows or hippopotami; and your cedar chairs capped with the winged solar disk, and your cedar stools supported by duck heads, and your ceremonial walking sticks figured with fine miniature portraits of your enemies . . . Of these walking sticks one alone was of plain wood: but this special cane, reverently laid away in a case of gold and electrum, was inscribed, "Wood which his Majesty cut with his own hand." It seemed an odd human touch, this reminder that the lord of so much glory was a youngster who enjoyed whittling wood.

And that of course was but a beginning of the vast, the incredible, catalogue. We observed also, in the rotogravure sections, throughout the while that your tomb was being slowly and scientifically robbed, your drinking cups and your bows and arrows; your fans, your finger rings, and your belt buckles; your gloves and your reading lamps, with

34

the wicks yet in them. We appraised your complete provisions, in short, for a continuance, in the Fields of Ialu, of that style of housekeeping to which you had been accustomed on earth, some thirteen hundred and sixty-odd years before the Christian era began its odd starting, four years after Christ's birth; and we noted also sundry discreet—but un-illustrated—hints as to your contraceptive devices, which, with unusual forethought, you had prepared against commerce with supernal concubines.

Finally you also were disinterred from your coffin of quartzite and pink granite, in order that your embalmed body might appear everywhere, upon terms of equality with the heaped wreckage of a tornado; and with the current visiting British author; and with scenes from the latest moving picture; and with the bared teeth, the regrettable legs, of the then regnant President's wife; and with extensive ginger ale advertisements: the each one of these presented to us in the same brown-and-sepia, and smudged, and sticky, and rather curious smelling form of publicity. There were songs made about you; and jokes about you also appeared in the allegedly humorous magazines. Columnists thrived opulently upon Tutankhamen for many months. Your despoiled corpse was placed on view in the Cairo Museum, as an exhibit of universal interest. Altogether, Sun of this World's Sky, you attained to an apotheosis unforetold anywhere in those four hundred and fifty chapters of *The Book of the Dead* which had been buried with you to serve as your Baedeker in the appointed journey toward the divine Fields of Ialu.

*

*   *

Yet about you yourself, the most widely known of all Pharaohs, we do not know anything, as a flesh-and-blood human being. You were but a child of eleven when you became Lord of the Two Lands; and at eighteen you died, it is believed, of tuberculosis. You married a daughter of that distinguished religious fanatic Amenophis the Fourth, that primal version of William Jennings Bryan, who was called Akhenaton. You succeeded him, and you repudiated his heresies, at we do not

To Tutankhamen

know whose dictates. And you yourself were succeeded, for a little while, by Ai, the Chief Priest and your Court Chamberlain, after whom reigned the great Horemheb.

This much alone we have learned about that Tutankhamen who is the most generally famous of the Pharaohs. You do not appear to have done anything whatever. No lad of eighteen, in brief, ever became a leading celebrity of the twentieth century with less personal effort; and to no human being did a world-wide fame ever arrive more belatedly. These facts are your sole and your sorry distinction, and yet for all that, Sun of this World's Sky, they remain an unique distinction in our planet's story and a fine triumph of injustice. The large achievements of Akhenaton and Horemheb are as though they had never been. But you, the callow, the mere void spacing between these superb careers, survive both of them, as a valued and celebrated museum piece.

So to you, Tutankhamen, the most shadowy of all famous persons whose names have become a proverb, I despatch my respectful greetings. For exceedingly wide glory you have possessed in my day, and in your day also you had no equal upon earth, in that dim time which we cannot quite imagine, not even with your complete household furnishings to aid us, when you were Lord over the Two Lands.

Then being but a child, you were led into great Amen's temple at Thebes: to your tiny chin they had affixed a false beard of gold turning upward at the end. The priest of Horus was masked as a hawk. Looking down at the perturbed small boy, he addressed his monarch in due form, declaring,—

"I bind the Two Lands beneath thee, at thy feet, so that the barbarians of Nubia and the tribes of Ethiopia may serve thee forever and thy majesty may be made eternal."

Then said the priest of Set, who was masked as a grayhound: "O my son, Lord of the Crowns, Tutankhamen, I bind the Lotus and the Papyrus for thee, I bring to thee dominion over the Two Lands. All the countries of the plains and of the mountains shall rest quietly under the feet of thy majesty forever."

In this way did you become Pharaoh, a visible god among mankind: and one cannot but wonder

what, in these unfamiliar and nightmarish surroundings, a small lean boy of eleven may have
thought about your deification.

*

*　　　*

Thereafter you breathed and ate by day, and at
night you slept. You signed with your cartouche
such documents as Ai brought to you. Your fame
was stupendous: all foreigners, as was widely remarked by the poets of the Two Lands, trembled
at a bare mention of your name. Your doings were
magnificent. One day, while playing in a forest,
you cut and trimmed neatly a walking stick with
your own divine hands, unaided. All they who approached you knelt, saying,—

"I am the servant of Pharaoh, the dog of his
house."

The amenities of social correspondence were, of
course, somewhat more formal. A properly bred
person began any letter to Tutankhamen, Lord
of the Two Lands, with the exordium,—

"I, So-and-so of the city Such-and-such, your
slave, the dust of your feet, the ground on which

39

you tread, your footstool, and the hind hoof of your sorriest horse, roll upon my belly and my back seven times at the divine toes of Pharaoh, the Sun of this World's Sky, humbly declaring, &c., &c."

Despite these civilities, you began to cough to a degree somewhat excessive for a god who is above mortal ills. You continued to lose flesh. You died.

*

* *

The embalmers dealt with you. The result of their art they placed in a golden coffin. The priests of Amen then wrapped this coffin in a silk sheet, strewing it with garlands of flowers. The priests of Horus laid it in a second coffin of gold inset with jasper and turquoise. The priests of Set placed all in a third coffin plated with gold, above the head of which rose the head of a gold cobra protectingly.

Thus encased, you rode slowly toward your tomb in the Valley of Kings, in a wagon drawn by white bulls. Your priests slew these bulls, hacking them into fragments. They applied these fragments, along with bits of frankincense from the South

To Tutankhamen

Kingdom and bits of alum from the North Kingdom, to the gilded lips of your effigy upon the
outer mummy case. Then they buried you there,
with your thrones and your walking sticks and your
paraphernalia for your divine amours, well knowing that henceforward the boy Tutankhamen was
an ever-living god dwelling in the fair Fields of Ialu.

They sealed up the door of your tomb. Afterward they went away from the Valley of Kings,
chaunting, as they were bidden to do, by *The
Book of the Dead,* "Thy annals shall be renewed."
But a few, if any, of these priests knew that they
were singing, through an unpardonable anachron-
ism, about the rotogravure sections in our Sunday
newspapers.

THE THIRD LETTER:

To Solomon, King over Israel

"The acts of Solomon, and all that he did, and his wisdom, are they not written in the book of the acts of Solomon?"

THE THIRD LETTER:

To Solomon, King over Israel

We of our country and faith, Great Son of David (upon whom be the Peace) preserve loyally the belief that Solomon was the most wise of mankind; yet as to this wisdom's demonstration do our records remain scanty and remarkably unconvincing.

In our Bible we are afforded, at utmost, just one display of this wisdom—in your decision, Light of the Age, between the two women who disputed over the possession of a child. . . . Well, and that anecdote, by ill luck, a bit blatantly disregards human nature, because one does not at all understand upon what principle (or through what extreme lack of it) the pretended mother preferred

45

to have the child divided in two. In brief, one dis-
trusts that anecdote.

Yet otherwise, O Most Mighty, we of these
western lands have but the cryptic assurance, in
our *First Book of the Kings*, that you were wiser
than Ethan the Ezrahite, or than Heman, or than
Chalcol, or than Darda—a statement which, inasmuch as we know nothing in particular about this
quartet, appears fairly non-conclusive. . . . No: it
may well be that the proofs of your wisdom were
written down among the acts of Solomon when
your yet other doings were catalogued, as we know,
in the Book of Nathan the Prophet, and in the
Prophecy of Ahijah the Shilonite, and in the Vis-
ions of Iddo the Seer; but we lack these literary
productions; and in our Bible, as we now have it,
you, O Sublimity, really do not display any
plethora of that wisdom with which the common
usage of mankind is at one to accredit you collo-
quially.

You builded the Temple, in which you by-and-
by did not worship. You were visited by the Queen
of Sheba. You wrote books. You espoused seven
hundred wives, and you took unto yourself three
hundred concubines. You turned idolater. That,

To Solomon

in brief, is your Biblical record; and no one of
these doings, I would humbly submit to you, O
King of Kings, exhibits any earth-staggering
wisdom.

*

*   *

It is true that our Bible omits a vast number of
the great and strange deeds which were done by
you during the forty years that you reigned over
Israel. For these, we must turn to those more ample
biographies of your exploits which the Orient has
preserved and the Occident knows hardly at all:
such biographies will, as men say, in a trice, reveal
you to have been, if not the most wise, at any rate
the most widely experienced and the most peculiarly favored of Hebrew monarchs. The Lord God
Himself favored you peculiarly; and indeed, as a
token of His divine esteem, He sent to the third
King of Israel a seal ring. It was fetched down,
from underneath the celestial Throne, we are told,
by the archangel Michael in person. The Lord's
secret name was engraved at full length upon this

47

seal ring, within a shining five-pointed star made out of a gem which is found only in heaven: and this ring conferred upon its fortunate wearer supreme powers.

So the four angels who rule over the four winds served under you; and the four angels who rule over living creatures, these likewise tendered you their allegiance, appearing at your court in the forms severally of a lion, a serpent, an eagle, and a whale. The six hundred and thirty devils who plague mankind with disease were, during the halcyon days of your reign, to be seen publicly in Jerusalem, whither they, along with all other devils, had come to render their homage in person to King Solomon. You thriftily put them to work at building your Temple; and it must have been a rare treat to the townspeople to observe these extraordinary day laborers, some of whom had heads like peacocks adorned with the horns of a gazelle, and others the heads of Nubians with the ears of a donkey, and yet others the heads of lions with the snout of an elephant. Each one of them had bat's wings and the claws of a vulture; and all were more or less covered with brilliantly tinted fish scales. Yes, I can well imagine that public in-

To Solomon

terest in the progress of the new Temple was considerable.

Moreover, all beasts and birds, and the various creatures of the sea likewise, served you because of your ring; and the power was granted you to converse with each one of these your subjects in its own language. There was not any power upon earth more great or more many-sided than the power of Solomon: but the extent of your wisdom remains, I protest, a quite different consideration.

*

*　　　*

At all events, you travelled extensively, on a magic carpet, into all quarters of earth—visiting, among other places, Mecca, where (as our Bible, yet again, fails to record) in the Kaaba you delivered a much-admired public address, prophesying the birth and the sublime mission of Mohammed. You overcame the rebellious fiend Sachr, at a particularly well-chosen moment, when the unconscious devil was lying dead drunk at the edge of a fountain. You were introduced by a

49

Ladies and Gentlemen

peewit to wise Balkis, the Queen of Sheba, with
whom your contest of wits resulted in a long line
of emperors over Abyssinia. You went into the
Valley of Apes. You mislaid your ring in a water-
closet, and you so lost your throne, becoming for
a while head cook to the King of Ammon; but
by-and-by you recovered this ring from the belly
of a fish which you were preparing for the King's
supper. And you had a great number of yet other
fine adventures, even until the moment when, at
the premature age of fifty-five, you expired in the
streets of Jerusalem, standing upright, and leaning
upon your staff—but were not observed to be dead
until an ant had eaten away the pith of this staff
so that it crumbled and your body fell down, an
exact year to the minute after your decease.

Yet during this busy while you, O King,
exhibited, to my judgment, very little more of
wisdom than you display in our Bible. To the
contrary, it appeared your métier to be outwitted
by pretty much everybody. Asmodeus got the better of you, and he got too the use of your entire
seraglio. The Queen of the Ants got the better of
you, as did also Markou, the King of Fools: a small
whale exposed you to public ridicule; and upon

50

To Solomon

various occasions a sparrow, a cock and a pigeon
made equally unbridled and unpunished fun of
King Solomon. But, above all, my dear fellow,
your women outwitted you, over and yet over
again. And at no time did you rebuke their duplici-
ties, or even argue about them.

*

*   *

It is a reflection which escorts me toward perturbed silence. I omit therefore to record the tricks
played on you, Splendor of the Universe, by
Nagsara, the daughter of Pharaoh; by Reblah, who
was daughter to the King of Gomer; by Glimith,
daughter to the King of Tubal; by Djarada,
daughter to the King of the Eastern Islands; by
Iamith, whose father was Emperor of the Sea-
Depths; and by a large number of those yet other
regally parented ladies whom you married, a bit
indiscriminately, upon seven hundred several
occasions.

For at this point it occurs to me that in dealing
with women your program was of great simplicity:

you permitted each one of them to have her own way. They required of you such matters as an image of loadstone, a sacrifice of burned grasshoppers, a palace builded of birds' bones; and without argument, you supplied each demand. They, as it were, piped: whereafter you danced—docilely, unabashedly, and even with some hint of amusement—in the high place of Chemosh. In brief, you did not ever reason with any one of your women: instead, you shrugged and gave in. The results were iniquitous, perhaps; but they nevertheless did preserve peace in your household, of seven hundred wives and of three hundred concubines.

It follows that, upon reflection, O Effulgency of the East, I do not doubt you thought the Lord God was a great deal more apt to be reasonable about your backslidings than was your seraglio to condone any distasteful intrusion of common-sense. And I begin now to wonder if this may not perhaps be the true meaning of your story: that Solomon was esteemed to be the wisest of humankind because at no time did he ever argue with his wife. I do not know, Fountain of All Magnanimity,

To Solomon

I do not even pretend to know. I would but present this hypothesis as the sole possible way in which married persons, of both sexes, nobody contradicting, can at least plausibly explain your world-wide repute for wisdom.

THE FOURTH LETTER:

To Egeria, the Fond Huntress

"Because he had been admitted to celestial wedlock, in the love and converse of the goddess Egeria, he attained to blessedness and divine wisdom."

THE FOURTH LETTER:

To Egeria, the Fond Huntress

As a figure of speech, Egeria, you have waned sadly. You smack somewhat of the eighteenth century, of Fox, of Burke, of Wellington: and Mr. Jefferson at Monticello, I do not doubt, referred upon fit occasion to the Egerias of Mr. Hamilton and of Colonel Burr in tones of polite malice. Even down to our grandfathers' day it was not uncustomary to remark, with sly nods, about this or the other successful male, "He has his Egeria"— and the phrase meant, of course, that woman in the background to whose counsels the man owed his worldly achievements. Nowadays we are apt to describe her influence more bluntly, in this or the other Anglo-Saxon term as little leaning toward elegance, Egeria, as did you yourself at the beginning of your incredible career in our world.

Yet no less vainly than for hens' teeth or for the Sirens' lost song may we seek for your exact start in life. It is known only that in the great forest of Nemi, among the Alban hills, you reigned as one of a dim and spectral trinity, in the same while that Solomon ruled over his more cosmopolitan Israel. Your associates in divinity at this time were Diana of the Woods and Virbius, that god who, as some said, had once been the mortal Hippolytus, the son of Theseus. These two were harsh and implacable deities, delighting to slay men and beasts alike, and valuing above all other virtues chastity. But you, Egeria, were a great deal more broadminded as to this point. You had smiled upward, very gratefully, toward divers flushed and tired mortal lovers, it was known; of many men were you the fond huntress; and the Aricians reported that their compassionate Egeria extended her ready charity toward women likewise, rejoicing to ease the pangs of childbirth with her kindly magic.

It is all cloudedly dim and far away. You are but an amorous and beneficent wraith moving among centuries of unrecorded quiet rustic happenings, to begin with; and you were thus quite an elderly, country-bred and robust, fine-looking rapscallion of a goddess when Romulus builded the first modest walls of Rome, over which Remus leaped with fratricidal results. Then you, Egeria, you alone of the Old Gods, you foresaw somehow the possibilities of this parvenu little Rome. And you removed from your upland forests to the suburbs of this small city, establishing your new residence in a magic grove just outside the Porta Capena, and fetching with you your current Sabine lover, one Numa Pompilius.

*

* *

So for the first time do you approach the outskirts of history, leaving Diana Nemorensis and Virbius to their cold woodland delights (and, a bit later, to the loving scholarship of Sir James George Frazer, in the I forget how many volumes of *The Golden Bough*) in order that you might enter more intimately into the amiable and blundering life of mankind. One does not recall any

59

other goddess who thus forsook her native mythology, bag and baggage; and who started life all over again, in brand-new surroundings, on a remarkably different footing.

For you gave up being worshipped also. You alone of the Old Gods decided—we do not know why—that it was not worth your while to be worshipped. You left abruptly your rude forest shrines in Aricia; and in your rather more urban new residence, beside the Tiber, you demanded no temples, no sacrifices, no prayers, and in brief no devout attention whatever from the run of mankind, now that you had your Numa Pompilius always directly under your eye and your thumb. In this way did you become the first female in all history to step down from your pedestal quite actually. You gave up godhead in order to devote yourself to the advancement of Numa Pompilius and the creation of Rome.

Well, but my theme here becomes, for one instant, delicate. It really is an odd fact, Egeria, that so soon as you became interested in Numa, his wife Tatia very conveniently died. It is yet another odd fact that so soon as you had established your Numa at Cures, Romulus conveniently vanished,

To Egeria

leaving vacant the kingship of Rome. I would not
for one moment suggest, I assure you, that you
had any share in either occurrence; your kindness
was notable: still, one does doubt if your kindness
was ever quite so great as was at all times your
exceedingly clear sense of just what you wanted.

Saying this, I cough and pass on. I assert merely
that while there were several candidates for the
kingship of Rome, only one of them was endorsed
by a former goddess. It followed that the Romans
—somehow—elected to be their second king a
peculiarly mild-mannered and harmless and hand-
some person who was not even a Roman, but a
Sabine. His name happened to be Numa Pompilius; and to this Numa you (who had never
bothered about such formalities in the free and
easy life of Nemi) were now married in complete
respectability.

*

*   *

Thereafter you took charge of matters single-
handed. Nowhere in the neighborhood of Rome

61

was any more nonsense talked about war for the next forty years. For the next forty years, punctually every evening, Numa repaired to your grove for the lawful delights of matrimony, including your instructions for his following day's work. . . . And the Romans obeyed their King Numa as docilely as he you. "He has," they said, "his Egeria" —and in your wisdom they placed entire confidence. So everybody did exactly as you decreed; and in consequence of this sensible behavior everything went nicely.

First you organized Rome's pantheon, naming at your own good pleasure such gods as you considered to be in reputable divine standing; you dictated what temples should be builded to these gods, and you carefully went over the architects' plans with an eye to economy; you appointed the necessary priests, allotting to them fair but by no means exorbitant salaries; and you thriftily cut down the sacrifices of those gods whose worship you had permitted, to an inexpensive offering of flour or of honey or of wine. Religion was essential and all that, you remarked, but there was no need to be wasteful about it. You composed also a code of common law which was based, by a startling legal innovation, entirely upon common-sense. You wrote a common-sense system of philosophy; and you had it declared official. You divided the citizens into guilds; and removing the soldiers of Romulus from the pension rolls, you set them to farming.

In brief, Egeria, there was no end to your bustling utilitarian activities during the forty years wherein you organized the complete social structure of Rome; got it to working nicely; put up with no nonsense from anybody; and affably supervised every least detail of Rome's government, like a benevolent, brisk, eternally young grandmother to the entire community. You took over in this way a village, and you turned it into an efficiently conducted kingdom, which survived and grew steadily, so that Rome became the first and the most great product of feminine common-sense.

Meanwhile you were sincerely fond of your meek Numa, I do not doubt, in your own bustling and I hope not too flagrantly patronizing fashion: but the mild, plump childlike man, after all, was mortal; and he thus grew older and thinner, and by-and-by undeniably more feeble, during those halcyon forty years, until at last he died tranquilly of old age. . . . And it was, one obscurely feels, an illogical relief to Numa Pompilius to be rid once for all of that benevolent tyranny which had kept him prosperous and famous and contented throughout forty years. . . . In any event, you then departed from the Rome which you had invented, and which, as you left it, was working smoothly, like a highly efficient machine in perfect condition. Men promptly began to try their hand at improving your huge creation; and of course they did disorganize it more or less; but in the main, this great feminine invention, the strictly common-sense polity of Rome, ran on smoothly enough in spite of over-much masculine meddling.

*

* *

But you, an immortal, the fond huntress, you who had found respectable married life so directly suited to your nature, you departed into Scotland, where you forthwith married Prince Florimont of Albania. Alas, Egeria, after mild Numa, you discovered the shrewd, the slightly penurious Gaelic temperament to be wholly uncongenial. You preferred to do your own economizing. You therefore quitted your Florimont posthaste, in unpleasant circumstances which it is not necessary to rehearse: and after that you began, like Solomon, to marry a bit at random, and for a century or two even a shade recklessly, in all quarters of the planet, without ever hunting down a man who proved endurable after the first few months of captivity.

Indeed, the pig-headedness of your husband, whose name was all but Legion, became rather discouraging. You could find nowhere upon earth, it seemed, any such dear and dependable milksop as was Numa Pompilius: instead, because of your never-failing optimism and your kindly nature, you found yourself perpetually being married to the most absurd sort of big-muscled and hairy creatures who spluttered and who banged upon tables in the throes of what they were pleased to call "being sensible." . . . At least one of these husbands was a Pharaoh, by whom you became the mother of Nectanebes the Second, and the grandmother of Alexander the Great: but your Pharaoh, too, you at last abandoned, with a not really ill-tempered shrug.

Ladies and Gentlemen

It was merely that, after being happily mated with a gentle and obedient and sensible Numa, no other husband could be regarded as a success. They argued matters, instead of doing as they were told for their own good; they had no real talents for docility; and their hardheadedness, after some six centuries of fond huntership for your Numa's suitable successor, so disgusted you with mankind that you virtually gave up marrying for an appreciable while.

*

*   *

Indeed, in a spasm of indignant widowhood, you retired to the island of Cephalonia. The matrimonial career of the fond huntress, it seemed to you, was at an end. There was no second Numa. One could but make the best of that fact. And then once again, Egeria, once more did your eternal optimism triumph over all your experience and over your sad memories of male obstinacy.

For you were visited in Cephalonia by a most captivating young Roman, named Gaius Julius

To Egeria

Cæsar, then on his way into Thessaly to contend with Gnæus Pompeius for earth's mastership; and to Cæsar you, like all the rest of the world, succumbed, making him also your husband. Yet only for a brief while, Egeria: for this hook-nosed young Cæsar, howsoever delightful as a lover, he too proved after marriage to have distinct notions of his own. When his wife told him quite plainly what she desired done, this illogical youngster would make open objections; and he would even argue the matter, almost in the insane tone of one who believes men to be rational beings.

No: there was really no putting up with the creature, not by anybody who remembered Numa. So you sent Cæsar packing, to fight Pompey at Pharsalia, and to take over the Rome which you had created some seven centuries earlier, and to make a sad ruin of your trim taskwork with his messy wars and his dictatorial manners and his general male slipshodness.

Nevertheless was it your dear consolation that Cæsar had left you in, as they say, an interesting condition, of which the upshot was a gratifyingly meek-natured boy, a dwarf, with an undeniable hump, but a most lovely face. Him you named

Ladies and Gentlemen

Oberon. With your deformed, beloved child you cannily went into Fairyland on that Friday night when the pagan oracles cried out, "Great Pan is dead!" and mortality of a sudden touched threateningly all the Old Gods. So did the Christian era, by an odd turn, restore to you, who had once been a heathen goddess, your long-lost former estate; and through the redemption of mankind you were made once more the benevolent, the brisk, but the no longer eternally young grandmother to an entire community. . . . For you so contrived matters, of course, that your dwarfed son Oberon was chosen to be king over your new country. The other candidates had no chance whatever against the electioneering abilities of an Egeria.

*

*   *

Thereafter, as you had once created the common-sense régime of old Rome, so now, just as lovingly, did you create the glittering nonsense of Fairyland. You abandoned realism as utterly as if

68

To Egeria

you had been legally wedded to realism; and you became an inventress of high romance. In the King's gold-roofed palace at Mommur, Oberon and Titania, whom you had picked out to be his wife, and regarded with grim disapproval, reigned most gloriously: but it was known that the true ruler of Fairyland was the brisk, bright-eyed gray-haired Queen Dowager. . . . It was for this reason that the Elves trusted Oberon implicitly. "He has," they said, "his Egeria." And all the Little People very well understood it was Queen Egeria who attended to the really practical side of their land's polity, sending to each royal christening a suitable delegation of well-disposed or malevolent fairy godmothers; providing every young male adventurer with his due assignment of wonder-working talismans; and endowing all properly approached beasts with the gift of human speech.

The Queen-Mother's main pride, the Elves said, was in her dragon run back of the palace, where she reared monsters of incredible magnificence; but with unicorns too she had a neat hand, and her ogres were justly famous. In brief, Egeria, it is known that you took over Fairyland, and devised for it a code of common law and a philosophy and a social ordering in very little imitative of your earlier labors in sociology. Meanwhile everybody did exactly as you decreed; and in consequence of this sensible behavior everything went nicely.

For now that age had begun to touch you forever increasingly, as it beset all the Old Gods when the Crucifixion was accomplished—with age, Egeria, you, even high-spirited and all-loving you, had matured in your irascible judgment more mellowly. Law and order and tranquillity and neatness were what people ought to delight in: but for some reason or another, male creatures lacked common-sense, and they hankered always (as no woman did, thank goodness, not even that scatter-brained Titania) for more gaudily colored playthings. Law and order and tranquillity and neatness did not content masculine beings. . . . Well, but it hardly mattered, after all, what foolishness these men might be up to during the brief time of their existence, said the fond huntress shruggingly. One might, it was an odd thought, one might, during those quarrelsome seven hundred years, one might better, perhaps, have been patient with that irrationality to which all men were born willy-nilly. . . . In short, if they wanted nonsense, you debated—not in your shrewd brain, Egeria, but in your huge grandmotherly heart—then why not give it to them?

Poor Numa, for example, the one really satisfactory husband whom you had ever found among so many hundreds of husbands, even Numa would have been more interested, after all, by a fine dragon than by a sound system of agrarian development. He would have derived more pleasure, it was an actual fact, from an evening of silly and sweaty copulation with one of the blonde princesses of your Fairyland than he did from organizing that so much needed College of Vestal Virgins on an efficient businesslike basis. And thus, nowadays, in looking back, it seemed rather a pity that you had ever forced the dear, mild, childish chuckle-headed creature, in defiance of his male instincts, to conduct himself sensibly and usefully. . . . Well, but one lived and learned. Not even an Egeria could always know what was really best for her protégé.

Meanwhile a third prince, you observed, had just started out, from over yonder in Poictesme, upon his quest of something or other. Quite a nice looking boy, too. He reminded you vaguely of

71

some long-legged and some long dead good-for-nothing rascal, whom you had probably married once, you reflected, as you glanced up smilingly from your industrious, trim, steady, indefatigable stitching, on a wishing cap.

So you put by your sewing, Egeria. And then standing up (a bit stiffly, a trifle rheumatically, nowadays, Egeria) you hobbled off back of the King's palace, and loosed one of your very finest dragons, to afford the lad a little harmless diversion.

THE FIFTH LETTER:

*To Jonah-ben-Amittai of Gath-
Heper, of the House of Jacob*

"God repented of the evil that He had said He would do unto them, and He did it not. It displeased Jonah exceedingly."

THE FIFTH LETTER:

To Jonah-ben-Amittai of Gath-Heper,

of the House of Jacob

The notion survives among us, Jonah, that you were treated a bit unconscionably in high quarters. Yet, if you also feel that your Employer displayed a certain instability—not here to call it obtuseness, —or that He evaded His share of a bargain which, if not ever formally ratified, was at least a moral obligation, nevertheless may you rest content, now that time has avenged you, very prodigally.

You had sought in all possible ways, as one recalls your story, to avoid the sad honor of becoming a celestial envoy to announce the impending destruction of Nineveh. You were haled back from your attempted evasion; embarked upon the most famous sea voyage in history; and compelled to deliver a prophecy of which both your philanthropy and your common-sense disapproved. Thereafter the people of Nineveh retired each family to their own ash-heap, and piously sat down upon it. Your Employer (drawing, one infers, some natural conclusions as to the mental gifts which prompted this special form of worship) decided not to plague any further "a city wherein are more than sixscore persons that cannot discern between their right hand and their left hand; and also much cattle." Upon this abrupt, this oddly bucolic note, your story ends; and you vanish from human knowledge after having been discredited by your mutable-minded Employer.

In this fashion were you compelled to set up unwillingly as a prophet, and forthwith deprived of all future prospects as a prophet. Apart from one very dubious reference, in *The Second Book of the Kings*, it is not recorded that you had ever foretold anything before your enforced *faux pas* in dealing with Nineveh: it is self-evident that when the destruction of this city failed to take place as announced, you could no longer hope to be regarded seriously as a soothsayer. Your reputation, as must beyond any doubt have been made plain to

To Jonah-ben-Amittai

you by your aunts and your cousins, was destroyed utterly.

Yet, in the odd way these things fall about, your reputation has survived. Your name is familiar above that of any other prophet; and your fame thrives handsomely, if but as a simile. Jeremiah and Daniel one esteems to be your sole rivals among the prophets of the house of Jacob, and they are very far outdistanced. We may yet speak, upon rare occasions, of a "jeremiad"; and those of us who have cultivated no wholesome horror of the cliché may refer now and again, without incurring any fit punishment, to "a Daniel come to judgment." But daily does somebody describe this or the other acquaintance, or it may be himself, as "a Jonah." By so generous a margin is Jonah, the son of Amittai, made the most celebrated of the prophets of Israel "where fame most lives, even in the mouths of men."

*

*   *

It would no doubt surprise you to learn that when the unthinking prattle in this manner they

appraise you as synonymous with a being unblest,
and ill-starred, and unlucky in every chance-taking,
or, in fine, as we would say, "hoodooed." With "a
Jonah" (for so very strangely do giddyheads and
simple Simons misinterpret your story) the worst
always does come to the worst; and his one possible
avenue of escape is to jump from the frying-pan
into the fire.—Which means, in other terms, that
"a Jonah" is born with a wooden ladle in his mouth,
and lives in perpetual hot water, with a hornet's
nest or two forever about his ears; so that he finds
the ground crumbling under his feet in the while
he goes rapidly to the dogs, on his very last legs.
That, Sir, in the Oriental profusion of metaphor
which your profession favored, is what the unreflec-
tive mean nowadays by "a Jonah."

So is it that we cling to our human habit of mis-
construing most matters, and make of you, who
were thrice-blessed among the men of old time, a
synonym for calamity. That outcome appears
astounding; but it remains true, in the teeth of
your never-failing, your almost incredible good
luck, over which the considerate yet marvel. Did
you happen, for example, to go overboard at sea?
Out of the many millions who have met that fate,

To Jonah-ben-Amittai

for you alone a great fish was in attendance to see
that you suffered no hurt. It is rumored, I admit,
that your good fortune in this respect was once
equalled by Arion, a Greek music maker, and yet
again by a Hanoverian raconteur, one Baron Mun-
chausen; but neither of these gentry has back of
him the supreme authority of Holy Writ.

So too, through your ever-present good luck, was
your sole essay in prophecy a flat failure. That failure, as the wise see it, was for you a peculiar if somewhat blasphemous triumph, in that from the first
you had not believed in the destruction of Nineveh, whatsoever your Employer might believe; and
in that you alone put no faith in the prophecy which
you delivered under supernal compulsion. I do not
find that mortal scepticism ever went farther, or
was rewarded more pleasantly. For in the end you
turned out to have been right all along; and you
were allowed the prized human pleasure of remarking to your Employer, "Was not this my saying
when I was yet in my own country?"—or, as we
would translate it more modernly, "Well, but
didn't I tell You so?"

The question, in so far as we know, was not answered. Indeed, one does not see how it could have been, except with some illogical, if familiar, repartee in the form of leprosy or of lightning.

But above all, Jonah, your never-failing good luck served you most handsomely in that you were the one prophet who was permitted to retire from prophesying. One infers so, at least, since there was clearly no point to entrusting you with any further celestial messages after your public discrediting by Heaven. Before another prophecy by Jonah, the heathen would but have exchanged their heresies for snickers. Obviously, you must have been authorized to settle down in some more congenial pursuit; and to do that was all clear gain, for a sociable person of your trouble-shunning disposition. Prophets might be looked up to and respected, by the more superstitious, with something of that uneasy deference which we accord to Commissioners of Internal Revenue; but prophets could hardly hope to be popular or much sought after. Their official forecasts of the future were too depressing; their standards of propriety were not the sort of thing to which well-bred Canaanites were accustomed; and their language turned far too readily toward tropes such

To Jonah-ben-Amittai

as, in any mixed gathering, must seem an embarrassing social blunder to persons who at all honor the amenities of living.

*

*   *

So I do not imagine that Isaiah and Amos and Ezekiel, or any other of those extreme faddists, were asked out a great deal. It could not have made for polite sociability, to have a guest remarking, at every instant, that the heavens were about to be rolled up as a curtain and the stars tumbled therefrom like rotted figs; that the fierce anger of Jahveh was preparing to forsake His covert, as a young lion, and to leave desolate all the land; that the best-thought-of people would very shortly become an astonishment, a hissing and a curse; and that, in brief, the Lord God of Sabaoth was making all needful arrangements to descend on the community at large like a bear that is bereaved of her whelps. I daresay Israel, as a whole, did not take her prophets seriously; no country ever does; but none the less, talk of this nature has its depressing aspect. Even if true, it was tactless. It was not the sort of tirade

81

which any upper-class Hebraic hostess would encourage by repeating any invitation to the fanatic
who had indulged in it at her dinner table. The
prophets, in fine, must necessarily have been distinct social failures.

Nor can I think that their private lives were of a
particularly happy complexion. To be the wife of
a Hebrew prophet, I suspect, was not an enviable
lot. We do not, of course, know just who among
the prophets were married. We know only that
your colleague Hosea was married; and we know
too that the wife of Hosea observed, by-and-by, "I
will go and return to my first husband; for then it
was better with me than now." Indeed, one does not
see how Gomer the daughter of Diblaim could well
have thought otherwise, after considering the frank
insults which her husband—at your Employer's
expressed command, Jonah—requested her two
younger children to repeat to her, in addition to
Hosea's divinely prompted bluster about stripping
her naked and slaying her with thirst. Marital observations of this sort, whatsoever may be their
value as parables, simply do not make for peace
in the home circle if a woman has any self-respect
in her nature and a tongue in her head. . . . Nor

To Jonah-ben-Amittai

of course, with a helpmate whose talk ran perpetually upon whoredoms and upon fornications and
upon sodomy and upon harlots and upon bruised
teats and upon women in travail and upon the
secret parts of both sexes, had the wife of a Hebrew
prophet, howsoever well reared herself, any least
chance to bring up her own children in a proper
state of biological ignorance. . . . No; one does
not envy the lot of a Hebrew prophet's wife, with
whom Jahveh was virtually a member of the family.
And one is certain that you, Jonah, were the most
lucky of all prophets, in that you failed completely
at outset, and were thus rescued from a profession
in which no philanthropic or peace-loving person
could hope to find real contentment.

❋

❋   ❋

For the rest, if at odd times in your later life some
bitterness rankled, when you thought over the con-
tretemps in which you had been involved willy-
nilly, you would nowadays, I think, incline to over-
look the affair magnanimously. In fact, I am afraid

that, knowing everything, you would grin. For the method employed to coerce you has turned out to be a strategic blunder of prime and perpetual importance. I refer, of course, to that great fish in whose belly you were incarcerated, and set to psalm-making.

Your fish, Jonah (as I fear, in the current state of human nature, it would rejoice you to learn) has been the unfailing delight of irreverence, and the mainstay of the village atheist, for a huge number of centuries. The half-educated everywhere have declined to swallow your fish, quite as resolutely as they have declined to stop talking about your fish. As in metaphor you outrank your compeers, so among all creatures of the deep is your great fish the most famous—and especially with those persons who have followed after you (if but at a considerable distance) in scepticism. Voltaire has made superb play with your fish; with Thomas Paine also was your fish a familiar pet; and your fish frolicked constantly among the torrents of the late Colonel Robert G. Ingersoll's eloquence.

But I desist here from any vain cataloguing of your disciples in unbelief. It is beyond arithmetic to estimate how many over-rational persons have

To Jonah-ben-Amittai

gagged gaily at Jonah's fish. Even the clergy approach it as though it were a bit fishy. I would but
assure you, Jonah, that if there be any topic of
which your Employer has very long ago wearied,
and before which, it is conceivable, He somewhat
colors up, it must be that great fish which in a misguided moment He borrowed from Babylonian
mythology, and sent to include you. That He regrets the entire affair, there can be no possible
doubt, now that this fish has so far parted with
every piscine attribute as to become a thorn in the
side of the devout, a stumbling-block for the feet
of the convert, and a pea-shooter in the ever-nimble
hands of agnosticism.

In imagination, O son of Amittai, I can see you
weighing the outcome of your ichthyological jail-
ing. By the beard of the prophet your grin is not
hidden to an extent quite consistent with utter
politeness. And I infer that of your Employer you
are perhaps asking, yet again, "Well, but didn't I
tell You so?"

THE SIXTH LETTER:

To Gaius Julius Cæsar, Dictator, Consul, Flamen Dialis, Scriptor,
&c., &c., &c.

"If thou consider rightly of the matter
Cæsar has had great wrong."

THE SIXTH LETTER:

To Gaius Julius Cæsar, Dictator, Consul, Flamen Dialis, Scriptor, &c., &c., &c.

When they crowded about you, Cæsar, the last faces which you saw upon earth, and in the chill March sunlight three and twenty knives were a-glitter—waveringly, in a confused onset, so perturbed by their victim's greatness that your half-panic-stricken murderers cut and mangled not only you but one another also,—then there was yet time to enrich the back of the dictionary with one more classical quotation. You seized that chance, you who let slip few chances. You cried out, in the instant that Marcus Brutus, your youthful well-loved protégé, was seen to have drawn his sword against you, "And you also,—my son, Brutus!"

That, Cæsar, was finely said. Than this brief

89

Ladies and Gentlemen

acknowledgment of paternity, in these exact circumstances, nothing could have been more dramatic, more simple, more poignant, or more easily memorable—which, after all, is a chief point to be regarded by the great in selecting their dying words.

Thereafter, it is recorded, drawing up your robe before your face, you expired with extreme dignity, in the Senate House at Rome, in the precise centre of the terrene stage, before a large and select audience of earth's very foremost notabilities. With such neatness was all contrived that you fell just in front of Pompey's statue, like a proffered sacrifice to the *manes* of him from whom you had wrested the world. As you his destruction some four years earlier, so now he supervised yours. And to complete everything, Marcus Brutus, the child of that Servilia whom you had loved in youth, had been quite unwittingly your son until the instant he became your murderer. No death scene, in brief, was ever better stage managed than when chance in this adroit way led up to the superb exit you made from mortal living.

And yet time—which, in the cliché, at least, tests all—time has brushed aside your last words

To Gaius Julius Cæsar

(along with your once famous epigrams, "The die is cast" and "I came, I saw, I conquered") as an utterance in no deep sense characteristic. And chance, Cæsar, all-treacherous chance, has fostered among us doubt if upon this high occasion you did actually light on *le mot juste*. We have begun to feel that you who died with such savoir faire, at the bright crest of your fame and of earthly omnipotence, as an acknowledged immortal, ought to have foreseen a bit more clearly the nature of this immortality.

That your nescience was human, one grants,— and, indeed, it may have been unavoidable. Even had affairs so fallen out as to restrict you to a more trite ending, upon a leisurely death-bed of the sort favored by Lytton Strachey and regrettably futilized by his imitators, it appears doubtful that, in the customary three pages of reminiscences through which so very many famous persons have of late years travelled backward to infancy, you would have remembered to include your enduring achievement. To Cleopatra (who would by this time have been your fifth wife) and to your beloved Brutus, weeping at the bedside, you would have said, we know, something heroic and well-chosen and wholly adequate, with the tact of a skilled diplomat rising handsomely to the occasion. But it seems improbable that even then, in such more happily unhurried mortuary moments, Gaius Julius Cæsar would have remarked, "All Gaul is divided into three parts."

*

* *

Yet it is by these words, Cæsar, that you have been immortalized, by these words alone you are remembered among us. So unpredictable are fate's workings that, in our later and lesser times, we employ the political propaganda which you called your *Commentaries on the Gallic War* as a school book. And the simplicity of language with which, as became an accomplished politician, you were careful to address the unlettered, but voting, lower classes has well earned for you the distinction of being that Roman writer against whom our young may charge most hopefully in the opening skirmish with Latin syntax. Thus it is brought about that, no great while after learning that Jack Sprat could eat no fat and that George Washington cut down

To Gaius Julius Cæsar

a cherry-tree, each one of us, in the freely impressionable hours of childhood, acquires likewise the information that all Gaul is divided into three parts: and these maxims abide with us throughout life.

No one of us, Cæsar, at any future time forgets your initial statement—or, at any rate, the first part of it. (Many memories, I admit, do skid at "of which the Belgians" and so on.) We recall forever that it was Cæsar who said, "All Gaul is divided into three parts." Even those of us who remember nothing else about Cæsar cling fast to this apothegm. Somewhat vague may become our notions concerning Virgil or Horace, or concerning any other of those Romans who follow you in the classroom; but about you, even until our childhood has ripened into senility, there is not ever any least vagueness. You were the person who said, "All Gaul is divided into three parts." And through this aphorism you entered into perpetual fame, as irrelevantly as by saying "Open, sesame!" did Ali Baba enter into the robbers' cavern and perpetual wealth.

With what precise sentiments, one marvels, would you learn that your crowded life had flowered in the form of a textbook for schoolboys? and a book, too, of which, in the ultimate, they retain just seven words? Of those other Romans who trouble our childhood each was in some degree a professional writer; and for a writer to become a schoolbook is the supreme, if somewhat grotesque, apotheosis. Though Virgil and Horace and Catullus and Ovid very certainly did not address themselves to the schoolboy, yet in their graver moments they well knew that to his impatient attention must dwindle by-and-by the concern of mankind, as a whole, with all such writers as are humorously called immortal.

But you, Cæsar, can hardly at any time have thought of yourself as a mere writer, you who were master of a planet. You could not well have anticipated that for you, whom the Senate had officially created a god, awaited the quaint destiny of being recalled, in common with your fellow deity Jahveh, as the author of a world-famous book which no mature-minded person ever manages to read all the way through. It was utterly hidden from you that, very much as another great soldier, General Robert E. Lee, became a school-teacher after Appomattox, so in the same lands which your legions had once

94

To Gaius Julius Cæsar

overrun, you, Cæsar, would come by-and-by to ex-
plaining the gerundive and the ablative absolute.

You did not grasp, in brief, the true nature of
your immortality. You could not foresee that because of one hastily written bit of propaganda, but
above all because of one statement in your pam-
phlet, you would be remembered, after the passing
away of two thousand years, by all literate beings.

*

*   *

Nor may the pensive begrudge you, Cæsar, your
enduring fame: fame here was merited; for that in
the greatness of your multiform achievements, and
in the variousness of your talents, you exceeded all
other men who have worn mortality, appears hardly
disputable. In considering you, the one difficulty is
to light on any rôle in which Cæsar did not excel—
except, to be sure, in the ineffably minor rôle of
Egeria's husband. For you were not only the chief
executive, the world's king, and the military com-
mander who had led armies into all known countries, without ever finding defeat. One recalls that,

95

beginning life as a highly thought-of clergyman in the service of Jupiter Capitolinus, you became equally looked-up-to as a criminal lawyer, with an extensive practice, besides being famous as an orator; that you were a virtuoso of every liberal art, and the most popular of seducers among the less scrupulous sex, as well as among your own sex; that you were an applauded poet, a well-thought-of astronomer, and the peerless war correspondent of your day; that you were a conceded authority on sewerage, published a first-rate treatise upon rhetoric, and founded a dozen or two cities. All things, in brief, were possible to you, Cæsar, who wrote our calendar, as it were, with one hand, and organized the world's first police department with the other, in the same instant that you were being worshipped as a god, with your own private shrine, in the temple of Quirinus. Not even in the politician's most delicate art of embezzlement had you any serious rival.

This much, O lordliest of all humankind, one can recall idly, upon the spur of the moment, without bothering to consult Plutarch, or Suetonius, or any encyclopædia, so that a little research work may complete the list of your unexampled exploits. For

To Gaius Julius Cæsar

the point is that no one of these doings has mattered a bean's worth. Out of all this splendor, as the lean product of mankind's supreme achievement in the way of mortal living, survive just seven words; and the one earthly memento of the greatness of Gaius Julius Cæsar, the most versatile of human heroes, remains the not even true statement that all Gaul is divided into three parts.

THE SEVENTH LETTER:

To Ananias, Citizen of Jerusalem

"Brand him who will with base report,—
He shall be free from mine."

THE SEVENTH LETTER:

To Ananias, Citizen of Jerusalem

In whatsoever limbo you now abide, Ananias, all grace to you! May your peace be multiplied through knowledge of your exceeding glory! For of the citizens of Jerusalem there is none of more wide repute than is Ananias; in every land is his name rumored; even unto the far ends of earth has sped his fame.

I must add, a bit more prosaically, that your fame appears undeserved. We know of you only that you were an early convert to Christianity; that when, in the year 33, the Apostles inaugurated the ecclesiastical and since then ever-crescent ceremony of "taking up a collection," you sold an unspecified possession, bringing some part of its proceeds to the Apostles; and that Peter reproved you for not contributing the entire sales price, in such terms that you straightway fell down at his feet, and in place of your deficit yielded up the ghost. Upon this slender foundation has been builded, like an inverted huge pyramid, your enduring and your magnificent fame as the chief of earth's liars.

That outcome defies human reason. It is not recorded you spoke at all. You came forward merely, with your money, a proceeding which, it is my experience, many modern pastors regard with indulgence. There was no verbal, no outright, lie involved in the affair one way or the other: at utmost, your offence might be described, by the hypercritical, as *suppressio veri*, with a mild tacit tinge of *suggestio falsi*. And in passing, one really does think that St. Peter, who had adorned the early morning hours of the first Good Friday with three out-and-out, outrageous whoppers, might more graciously have ceded the task of criticizing your veracity to some other Apostle.

At all events, such was your entire story as it survives in six brief Biblical verses: and the considerate person (in a land where each of us annually fills out his Federal and State tax returns with the aid of much salutary self-abasement as to his earnings and worldly possessions) cannot but wonder over the titles of your pre-eminence. It is not that one envies you, exactly. Your glory arouses, rather, an odd mixture of surprise and memory, a slight flavor of contrition, and some sly self-complacency in having outrivalled you, Ananias, over and yet over again, without being caught at it.

We do not then plot to displace you in your ever-living fame, I can assure you. You incite nobody to any infraction of the tenth commandment. No: we do not presume to covet the great fame of Ananias. Instead, we remark humbly, provided that we are sound classical scholars, *Sic nos, non nobis.*

*

*   *

For by a deal more than Tutankhamen's does your celebrity appear unearned. He at least had his tomb to contribute to our era, as an unique phenomenon; but about you there was, in so far as our era knows, no suggestion of the unique, whether in your deeds or in your temporal gear or in your personal qualities. So of all them whose names have passed into proverb your case stays, by long odds, the most unexplainable; your claims upon our human attention are so tenuous that their bland inadequacy rivets our attention with firmness; and provokes the considerate to wonder upon what principle, if any principle, fame does choose her pets?

I refer thus to those people who are really famous, upon more or less the same gigantic scale as you, Ananias—to those favored and those ever-glorious dead who remain known to that unpedantic if semi-fabulous creature, the man in the street. For he—even that John Doe, who is himself a celebrity of sorts—even he is familiar with the entire alphabetful of them, from the Ananias who was a liar and the Amati who was a violin, down to the Volstead who was an act and the Zeppelin who was, and remains, a flying machine. Each one of us, in fact, knows all about the achievements of these most memorable persons. We very well know that King Alfred let his cakes burn, and Bruce looked at a spider, and Nebuchadnezzar ate grass, and Mahomet went to a mountain,—in or about that period, of course, when the Borgias poisoned, upon the same broad principle that King Henry the Eighth married, pretty much everyone within sight, while somewhere in the immediate neighborhood Nimrod was hunting, and William Tell shot at apples, and Nero combined music with arson.

But not only do we recount their names and their exploits. We cherish also each attribute of all these proverbial beings, even to their least personal possession, remembering no less reverently the mark of Cain than the coats of Joseph and Prince Albert, the line of Messrs. Mason and Dixon, and the locker of Davy Jones. We recall daily that Œdipus had a complex, Job a comforter (in addition to a blue turkey hen), Titian a blonde, Juliet a balcony, Bright a disease, and Monroe a doctrine, so great is our love for all those of our race who are undisputedly famous. In brief, these people who have aided mankind by contributing to our language a familiar allusion—a scant two hundred persons, it may be, out of the billions of unfeathered bipeds who have strutted at odd times about the planet—are actually and forever famous. Down "the great Mississippi of falsehood" they sail statelily, a multi-colored and a bewilderingly mixed crew, enlisted from all lands, all eras; and all travelling in the same huge gleaming galleon of romance.

*

*   *

Ah, but what, Ananias, one must ask perforce, are you doing in that galley? As a liar, your record remains, at best, obscure. It may be granted by the charitable that, for aught we know to the contrary, you did perhaps lie to the tax collectors of Tiberius, and to your wife Sapphira, with some traces of real ingenuity. Nevertheless were your talents for mendacity so inadequately bolstered by bravado that before the first hint of St. Peter's doubt you succumbed, in circumstances from which one bare "Cockadoodledoo!" would have loosed you triumphantly. To none thus insulse is it granted to win the victor's palm in the most ancient and human sport of perjury.

And so to you, Ananias, in whatsoever limbo you now abide, may grace be with you; but not—upon reflection—no, not that glory which, living, you did not earn, as so many others have earned in this flesh, with their tongues and their pens, tirelessly. For you were not ready of wit: you lacked any sprightly meed of imagination: you were but a pettifogger. In brief, I have no least doubt that Simon Peter, having been fulfilled with a knowledge of things to come, put a sudden destruction upon you, Ananias, not so much for being backward with your church dues as for being a humbug who was making ready to swindle the next nineteen hundred years of what we politely call civilization.

THE EIGHTH LETTER:

To Sir Galahad of the Siege Perilous

"When Sir Percival and Sir Bors saw Sir Galahad dead, then if they had not been nobly bred persons, they might lightly have fallen into despair."

THE EIGHTH LETTER:

To Sir Galahad of the Siege Perilous

We may still speak, fair Sir, of this or the other acquaintance as "a Galahad"; but never, I believe, until he is dead. In fact, the late Lord Tennyson's mathematics—by which your strength was figured out as equivalent to the strength of ten, because your heart was pure—have become a polite common-place in referring to any recently deceased person who did not actually die in jail; and the quotation remains a leading favorite in our obituary columns and upon tombstones. Meanwhile no as yet living mortal, I believe, has in any circumstances been described as "a Galahad," and most certainly, not ever to his face, if but because of our human doubts as to quite how he would take it. For the more care-

Ladies and Gentlemen

fully one considers your history, fair Sir, the more
dubious to one's thinking becomes its exact moral.

*

*   *

Matters were going well enough, upon the whole,
in King Arthur's England. The realm prospered as
a political unit. In the war against the Emperor
Lucius, the English army had overrun half Europe,
so triumphantly that the Pope's own hands had re-
crowned and consecrated Arthur in Rome, and the
Pope's bull had bestowed upon Arthur the fairly
generous title of Emperor over the Known World.
No foreign enemies now troubled Arthur Pendragon, because there was no monarch so great or
so foolish as to attempt battle with the all-conqueror. And internally, the affairs of England were
administered satisfactorily enough, from the gentry's point of view, by the King's will and by the
King's posse of those one hundred and forty-eight
knights who sat with him at the Round Table in
the Great Hall of Arthur's castle at Camelot.

These gentlemen were sworn "never to do out-
rageosity nor murder"; to fight in no wrongful

cause; to preserve loyally their personal virtues; always to grant clemency when it was asked; and to serve chastely and faithfully every gentlewoman who needed aid against giants or heathen or dragons or her nearer relatives or any other of this world's ills. It was an oath renewed annually at the high feast of Pentecost.

Being human, these gentlemen did not keep this oath in every particular. They discovered, for example, while travelling about the remoter and more bucolic shires on the King's business, that an occasional murder both sped the traveller's progress and helped fill his purse. The exact rightness of any cause, and the precise dictates of personal virtue, they found to be matters more conveniently talked over at leisure with one's priest, the next time one confessed, than settled, it might be in the wrong way, by oneself among the distractions of everyday life. There was, thus, no real hurry about any such highflown considerations. As for the service of gentlewomen, it was generally known at King Arthur's court in what capacity Sir Launcelot served Queen Guenevere, and Sir Tristram Queen Iseult, and Sir Lamorak Queen Margawse—upon which last-named lady, for that matter, King Arthur had begotten the dark-browed Mordred, despite the circumstance that Margawse was King Arthur's own sister. One did not openly discuss such affairs, it was true; but one knew about them; and one followed, of course, the example set by the best people.

So the knights of the Round Table, I take it, lived each man his own more or less self-seeking, more or less lecherous, and more or less abominable and unheroic private life; and enjoyed it tremendously. The magnificence of the court was unparallelled; money was plentiful; the tournaments were always good fun; the presiding ladies were all lovely and not the least bit prudish: and, in brief, the gentry of England frolicked in an era of unexampled prosperity.

Nevertheless at each Pentecost did the knights solemnly renew the oath of their office, and then they feasted together at the Round Table. Upon the King's chair and upon the chair of each knight was its owner's name engraved, in a fair diamond-bright lettering: one chair alone had remained, since the order's founding, uninscribed and vacant. For this was the famous Siege Perilous, which in due time would be occupied, said Merlin's prophecy, by "a knight that shall have a head of gold,

the look of a lion, a heart of steel; conditions without any wickedness, and the valor of a seraph, and
entire faith and belief in God the Father. And he
shall be the Best Knight in the World."

He would thus come as a messiah, the knights
knew, to be their leader and to restore complete
righteousness in England. That would be utterly
splendid. But, I have no least doubt, a considerable
number of these one hundred and forty-nine gentlemen reflected privately that there was no real hurry
about these highflown considerations, either. Matters were already going quite well enough—upon
the whole—in King Arthur's England.

*

* *

Ah, but by-and-by, Sir Galahad, you did come to
fulfill, the prophecy. Unarmed, young, grave, and
innocent of all earthly sin, you came into the King's
banner-hung hall, in your robe of ermine, the fur
of that beast which dies rather than endure any
smirching. You sat down tranquilly in the Siege
Perilous, a proceeding fatal to any other mortal

115

person. After that, you withdrew Balin's sword from the charmed block of rose-pink marble, when neither Gawain nor Percival, not even the huge-thewed Launcelot, was able to draw out this sword. Through such prodigies were you attested to be the long-looked-for Best Knight in the World.

So great indeed, Sir Galahad, was your holiness that when you next sat down at the Round Table, after the adventure of the sword, there came suddenly a peal of thunder, followed by a vast driving windstorm and complete darkness: then entered into King Arthur's feasting hall a ray of sunbeam more clear by seven times than is the sunlight of earth. In such blinding splendor did the knights see, veiled with a covering of white samite, the most holy Sangreal, that cup into which Christ's blood had been shed for their redemption. The cup vanished, leaving an odor of sweet spices.

By this miracle were these easy-going knights aroused to repentance over their lax manner of living. First the impetuous lewd Gawain, and then all the others, made a vow to set forth in quest of the Sangreal, and to behold unveiled the most holy object upon earth, or else to die in the pursuit of its holiness. Upon the morrow they, and you also,

To Sir Galahad

fair Sir, departed from Camelot, each gentleman taking the way that he liked best. The King alone of the Round Table remained in Camelot.

*

*   *

Thereafter you, Sir Galahad, and you only, achieved the quest of the Sangreal. It was an outcome well merited by your superb and countless virtues; but that outcome is not my immediate point. I am content herewith to take leave of you lying in state, as the dead king of the mystic city of Sarras, at the conclusion of your strange and most edifying adventures. I really cannot cry over you. I reserve, rather, my pity for your outrivalled fellow knights of the Round Table.

For outrivalled they were, very completely. Within a week or so, in fact, a few of them had straggled back to Camelot, disposed to laugh off the entire matter. "Christ died for our sins," they remarked, to every effect: "but, after all, that was a great while ago. We are now living, let it be remembered, in the sixth century, not in antiquity. The world does change, with all this modern progress

117

about, whether we want it to or not. Fact is, my dear, we live in an age of scepticism. Religion is very well in its way and in its proper place, and I am heartily in favor of it, do you not misunderstand me. Fact is, the lower classes could hardly get on without it. And of course, when everybody is a bit wrought up, a good sportsman does not like to stand out, and so you see how it was. He did it with mirrors, probably. Anyhow, nothing personal was intended, I can assure you, by those vows of eternal chastity. Fact is, if your husband has quite decided on that trip to Northgalis, I will drop in for supper next Thursday evening."

But a great number of these gentlemen did not ever come back. In their pursuit of the Sangreal they blundered into the most unconscionable giants and dragons, who left of them mere gobbets of chewed flesh; or they ventured so near, in their genial human iniquity, to the most holy Sangreal that its holiness slew them; or they encountered, in one or another foreign land, young women who married them resistlessly, and forthwith converted them into humdrum and quiet-living citizens of that country; or they lost heart, after repeated failure, and became anchorites in this or the other

To Sir Galahad

suitable foreign wilderness, seeking through eternal
penances to atone for their attested unworthiness
in the sight of high Heaven; or they met with, during their quest, some yet other conclusive doom,
about which their relatives and consoled heirs never
heard the exact circumstances. In brief, not over
many of this glorious if somewhat loose-living
brotherhood returned to resume knightly service
under King Arthur; and those who did return came
back as confessed failures.

*

*   *

Things were not ever quite the same again in
King Arthur's England. You had brought complete
holiness into the realm, fair Sir, and those whom
this holiness did not destroy, it, if but vaguely, had
discouraged. The Sangreal, "which is the secret of
Our Lord Jesus Christ," had passed a bit too uncomfortably near to them. That miracle had left
momentarily an odor of sweet spices everywhere
about one, and it had left, momentarily, a noble
desire and a high aspiring, not utterly grasped by
the mind. But it had left also an abiding sense of

not being quite in sympathy, after all, with complete holiness and of not—not quite—liking it. No,
it really was not—after all—not wholly the sort of
thing with which a gentleman could live, nowadays,
in exact comfort. . . . And yet, one felt too, perhaps
that absurd, young, beautiful, grave Galahad had
found in life an exceedingly great treasure which
one had missed, somehow, confound the young
idiot! . . . Well, but life was a sorry, a rather miry
sort of business; and in the actual working out of
human affairs overlofty ideals led to life's getting
the better of you. Sensible people would let them
alone. . . . Meanwhile the Sangreal was only a cup;
and one had plenty of cups, with a butler always
ready to fill them. And next Thursday her husband
was running over into Northgalis. Things might
have been worse.

*

*   *

"You have bereft me," said King Arthur, when
the quest of the Sangreal was cried, "of the fairest
fellowship and the truest of knighthood that ever
were seen together in any realm of the world." And

To Sir Galahad

the King spoke truly. After his knights had once
taken seriously the oath they made every year, and
had turned, at least temporarily, toward the pursuit
of superhuman perfection, matters did not ever
again go well in King Arthur's England. You left
him, Sir Galahad, with a weakened and discouraged
band of supporters, who were not any longer able
to fight for Arthur Pendragon in the former genial
and broad-minded spirit of compromise, or to support the chief's toplofty pretensions, bless the old
flannel-mouthed rascal, with a sly wink. So the
power of King Arthur crumbled, now that it was
bereft of the kindly aid of human humbug: and the
treason of Launcelot, the malignity of Mordred, and
Gawain's lack of self-control, all combined to complete—in that dim last battle fought confusedly in
the fog near Salisbury—the task which your un-
flawed virtue had begun at Camelot.

I do not know that any safe moral is possible. But
I do know, more or less, after thinking over your
story, why we elect never to describe any living person, to his face, as "a Galahad." We do not think it
civil to impute to any well-thought-of friend a supernal holiness which, at the bottom of our human
hearts, we do not really like or quite trust.

THE NINTH LETTER:

To Hamlet, King of Jutland

*"O good Horatio, what a wounded name,
Things standing thus unknown, shall live
behind me!"*

THE NINTH LETTER:

To Hamlet, King of Jutland

It is well, your Majesty, for us modern weaklings now and then to consider that directness of action and that lack of all hesitation which characterized your every doing. With us, thought has become a species of malady which leads to much time-wasting: we weigh, as we say, the pros and the cons, where you found never any chance for such nonsense. For indeed, when your depraved uncle, after murdering your father, and espousing your mother, had usurped the throne of Jutland, your position was highly dangerous. It was not healthful to be the legal heir in any such circumstances, with an uncle so purposeful. Prompt action was necessary: and in action, Sire, as you forthwith demonstrated, you excelled. Not many persons could have conceived and carried out the bold if a bit barbarous stratagems by which you despatched your uncle Fengon in his own turn, or could have improvised that stirring oration which you thereafter delivered to the people of Jutland, winning them at once to acclaim you their king.

Thereafter, having held your coronation in due estate, and having received "the homages and fidelities" of your subject Jutlanders, you set sail for England, where you married the King of that island's daughter. And in England your true troubles began, with a treachery which was followed by open warfare and by-and-by was capped with strange slanders. For your widowed father-in-law sent you into Scotland, nominally so that you might woo the land's Queen as his bride, but in reality to give her an occasion to murder you, as was the hard custom of her haughty courage in dealing with all men who talked about marriage.

Ah, but thereupon this Queen Hermetrude, "mocking at the old King of England's fond appetites, whose blood as then was half congealed, cast her eyes upon Hamlet, this young and pleasant Adonis of the North, esteeming herself happy to have such a prey fall into her hands." In brief, your Majesty, she smiled upon you, an ante-Longfellovian John Alden. The sole difference was that you did promptly speak for yourself, without further urgings. With that lack of shilly-shallying which distinguished you, Sire, you married Queen Hermetrude out of hand: whereafter you and your two wives and your cheated father-in-law lived tumultuously for the remainder of your reign, in an ever-bubbling hell-broth of complots and privy murders and pitched battles, into which at long last entered yet another one of your uncles (but upon the maternal side) with whom your Scots wife betrayed you.

*

* *

But it is not my purpose to recall to your Majesty's notice these far-off hearthside dissensions. They all ended a great while ago, as unpleasantly as do most family arguments, as finally as do all human lives. My point here is merely that your forthright and inspiring story was preserved in the now perished Skjöldunga saga, whence Saxo Grammaticus (a Danish historian, Sire) copied it toward the beginning of the thirteenth century: and from Saxo Grammaticus your ancient, inveterate enemies, the English, took over this story, at various removes, in order that they might convert it into stage plays which misrepresent your Majesty's conduct and nature and achievements to an extent truly remarkable.

You would pardon, it may be, as in some sort a flattery, that untruth which makes of your father the high King over all Denmark (even at an instant when your mother's father, King Rörek Slyngebond, was still enjoying this title). But to naught else in the story of Hamlet, as these English have everywhere mistold it, could you as a true Viking extend manly indulgence. That you, of all Jutlanders —you, the strong and cunning and unscrupulous and the always victorious champion, to whom a half-dozen or so killings were but a part of everyday's work—you, whom in our modern tongue we would nowadays describe, your Majesty, as the eighth century's leading "go-getter"—should be thus parodied as a philosophic John-a-Dreams is, in point of fact, an offence against which your own

To King Hamlet

people, no less wisely than explicitly, provided in
due form.

It is, I submit, a clear case of *tungunid*, or of
"tongue slander," which the laws of Jutland for-
bade to that land's better governed poets, by ordain-
ing:

"No man shall make *tungunid* on another, in
songs or in lampoons or in private talk. If it be
known that he has done this, he is liable to out-
lawry: he falls as an outlaw, without punishment
being incurred, if anyone slays him. No man shall
make exaggeration or misreport about another man,
by saying about another man what cannot take
place, or has not taken place, such as declaring he
is a woman every ninth night, or has borne a child,
or by calling him *gylvin* (which is, a she-wolf).
Such liars are outlaws: they fall as outlaws if they
be slain."

*

* *

That was the law in your Jutland, Sire: and the
fact leads me to wonder with just how much of

Northern phlegm you would hear, for example, of Goethe's bland declaration that your life exemplifies "a great deed laid upon a soul unequal to the performance of it. Here is an oak-tree planted in a costly vase which should have received into its bosom only lovely flowers; the roots spread out, the vase is shivered to pieces."

It would seem to you quite as far out of reason, one suspects, to call you a costly vase (with a bosom) as to call you a she-wolf: nor did your sense of duty ever assume quite the proportions of an oak-tree. With your ever-present need to get on successfully in a treacherous and hard-hitting world, you had rarely the time to think about duty. So against Goethe, and against all other persons who have written about you during the last three centuries, you would decree with a clear conscience, I think, the due punishments of proved *tungunid*. It is true your conscience had a digestion somewhat superb: and to hear anyone remark, for instance, "conscience doth make cowards of us all," would have seemed to you as supremely funny as to doubt, for one half-moment, that a Viking, after he had shuffled off this mortal coil, went straight to Valhalla as a mere matter of course. You did not bother, therefore, about whether it was better to be or not to be, because you meant, quite simply, to make the best of both worlds.

*

*   *

In fact, now I think of it, the whole affair would seem to you to be funny. You were a jovial enough ruffian, with a marked taste for practical jokes: and you might well see the point of this joke. For Hamlet to-day, some twelve centuries after your demise, is the best-known character in the world: and not one word which we know about him is true. Your fame, Sire, is world-wide and superb and completely mendacious. Not books but entire libraries have been written about your Majesty: and in none of these books do we find a syllable of truth recorded as to your conduct or your nature or your achievements.

I do not think you would greatly admire the rôle in which you appear before posterity; it has few of the Viking virtues. But I do think you would see the rich humor of this masquerade, and that you would delight heavily in the upshot of this *tungunid* by your ancient enemies, the English, this *tungunid* which has made Hamlet so much more famous than any skulking Englishman who ever lived to die a cow's death.

*

*   *

You yourself, it is known, were instructed, during your father's lifetime, in the dark arts of sorcery, "for in those days the North parts of the world, living as then under Satan's laws, were full of enchanters." You had, like every Viking monarch, your own personal magicians in daily attendance—your galdra-smiths, whose duty it was, for your convenience, to cure wounds and sickness, to subdue fires and storms, to raise up the dead to advise you, and to win for you the love of any desired woman. So it seems a great pity that, with two sorts of magic—both *galdr* and *seid*—in such constant practice in and about your court, their methods were not ever

132

To King Hamlet

utilized to procure for you, Sire, an advance copy of *Hamlet, Prince of Denmark.*

On a feast day you might then have somewhat varied the routine of entertainment—or so at least I imagine. I can see, or at any rate I appear to see, your Majesty throned in the high seat facing the sun, that seat which the King alone is permitted to occupy: it is carved with runes and the twelve signs of the zodiac, and the tall back of it is adorned with two dragons' heads, all brightly colored. You are clothed in a scarlet kirtle, over which you wear a fringed cloak of two colors, of alternate green and yellow. Around your sun-burned blond hair, which is parted in the middle, one observes a small gold band. Your feet rest upon clean straw, into which you drop the meat bones as you finish gnawing at them. You then lick your fingers carefully, for in decorum and personal habits you are neat, and even a bit finicky, as becomes the first gentleman of your realm.

On a bench at your left sit your two wives with their women attendants in the strict order of their rank. Before you are ranged your warriors upon longer and lower benches, with their shields and swords hanging upon the wall behind each man, ready at need. You have all dined heartily: the ale vat has thrice been brought into the hall and thrice emptied. The King's drinking horn is of bronze, and has a rim of silver ornamented in relief with the figures of reindeer. But the always cautious King does not drink much: thus far, he has vomited only once into the piled straw and meat bones.

The gleemen have entered with their harps and fiddles and *gigjar*, but in place of the customary poem or saga, to-day a skald crowned with mistletoe is declaiming, to the assembled company, from that advance copy of *Hamlet, Prince of Denmark*. You have listened reflectively. Your shrewd, gross, red, and much weather-beaten face has passed from suspicion to bewilderment, and thence to complacency. The entire story is new to you: Hela will punish in due season all such liars: meanwhile this insane saga seems nonsense likely enough to be believed in by the effeminate and underhand English, a people who try to murder their own sons-in-law, and thus force you to murder them. Only with the last act, when you hear of your pathetic death in early youth, and of your throne's passing to a practical man of action, do you give

134

way to outright mirth, holloaing jovially, slapping your knees, and uproariously breaking wind. For you well know that in all Jutland there is no Viking more strong or more cunning or more unscrupulous, or blessed with better luck in all his bloody endeavors, than is Hamlet the King.

THE TENTH LETTER:

To the Seignior Geoffrey Rudel,

Prince of Blaye-en-Saintonge

"Such questions of love casuistry are thoroughly characteristic of the social element in the troubadour poetry."

THE TENTH LETTER:

To the Seignior Geoffrey Rudel, Prince of

Blaye-en-Saintonge

Thus speak they, say they, and tell they the tale of your earthly venturings, Seignior, that tale of whose verity you may judge better than I. They narrate that you were a poet who made excellent sirventes, and tensons, and lais, and aubades, and sestinas, and still other verbal luxuries, being an apt practitioner in each branch of the Gay Science. You were likewise a prince, as yet young, lacking for nothing in pleasant meadow lands and strong castles, in your estates near Bordeaux; nor did you want for furred robes with snug hoods and tippets, or velvet doublets, or gold and silver plate, or fine riding horses. In person you were tall and well fashioned. You went glowingly, clothed in red or in green or in yellow, as became a chevalier, to whom all drab colors were forbidden. Your hair was brown, in little curls; your eyes also were brown, and bright, and meditative. You were beloved by a host of women, who reported that the pillow cases of your bed were of purple silk worked with gold threads.

To all women you were courteous, to many exalted ladies you rendered lip-service, praising them in neat songs for their small beauties, their undazzling virtues. But at all times your heart remembered that, in faraway Palestine, lived that Countess of Tripoli of whose beauty and whose virtues the crusaders and the monks and the pilgrims, returning from out of the Holy Land (which her presence made doubly holy) spoke unbelievable reports, and about whom they related noble tales not to be credited for one instant by anybody except a poet. You, Seignior, were a poet.

The reports of this lady's excellence, for this reason, came to you as mere confirmation of the knowledge with which all poets are born—that somewhere upon earth, waiting to be encountered at her own good hour, yet lives that woman in whom there is no imperfection, and whom one may

To Geoffrey Rudel

love utterly and deservedly. So did you become en-
amored of this Dame Mélisande whom you had
never seen. Your desire of her left room, in your
sumptuous and familiar life, for no zest: your desire
became a wasting malady. Your tall young body
sickened under its ardors, at that season of the year
when the green herbs and the leaves appear, and
white flowers bloom in the fields, and the nightin-
gale first lifts her voice.

It was then, they narrate, that you chartered a
ship, Seignior, and so came in due time to that
castle in Syria wherein your lady resided with her
six children and with her gray slow-speaking husband, Count Bertrand, then Lord of Tripoli, born
of the noble house of Toulouse. Through the hot
bright midday of that "land of sand and ruin and
gold" they brought you into the presence of Dame
Mélisande, lying upon a litter. You had but the
strength to touch her hand, in the while that you
said faintly:

"Most illustrious princess, my elect lady in
domnei, I will not complain of death. I have seen
you, and I have thus achieved the sole desire of my
life."

Ladies and Gentlemen

Thereafter you kissed her hand, and so died, the happiest lover, it was said by the intelligentsia of your era, in the whole world.

*

*　　*

Thus far, Seignior, should the tale be known to you, if the dead indeed remember their doings upon this planet. Whether any tidings reached you as to what happened afterward, no living man may guess; but beyond question this sequel would have rung sweetly in your ears, even among the harps and the lutes of your paradise. For you, Seignior, were a poet.

Your death, I must tell you, made a splendid stir in the polite world, which acclaimed you as a paragon of lovers in the very highest style of chivalry. The troubadours sang everywhere of Geoffrey Rudel, comparing you not unfavorably with Roland and Launcelot. Your fine song made in your lady's honor—*Irat et dolent,* and so on—became famous at every Court of Love. Your heart-hunger for your *"amor de luench"—la princesse lointaine,* the faraway princess—in contradistinction to the accessible women about you, was an apologue which all poets understood instantly, and have since cherished.

Meanwhile the Countess had caused your body to be magnificently buried, in the church of the Knights Templar at Tripoli. Your tomb was of porphyry, they record; and upon it were engraved verses, of your lady's own making, to commemorate your constancy and devotion.

"Ah, my fair friend Rudel," rhymed Dame Mélisande, "fear not that my heart shall ever elude you, or that I will ever accept another lover; for were a hundred barons to pursue me with amorous prayers, this love which holds me bound as your captive would compel me to keep my heart for you alone: and I must thus guard my body likewise, so that such an one as now enjoys it may nevermore possess the body of Rudel's lady in domnei."

Then speak they, say they, and tell they the tale that, so extreme was the grief of Dame Mélisande, she took eternal leave of her husband and of her six children. She entered a nunnery, to devote the remainder of her life to the service of Heaven and the memory of Prince Geoffrey Rudel. Such was your complete history, Seignior, about which Swin-

burne has written some superb verses, and Rostand
a rather so-so drama gemmed with pale lyrics.

*

*   *

I admit, Seignior, that in this tragedy my sym-
pathies turn toward your lady's husband. He, good
man, was nowhere consulted in this affair, which
upset his entire living, without granting him anywhere the chance to make even one heroic gesture.
A dying stranger is brought to the castle,—and ex-
pires there, within two minutes, after speaking some
unintelligible nonsense or other. Count Bertrand,
as an old soldier, could think but little of an inci-
dent so common in warfare; and he no doubt went
in to his delayed dinner that day with his accustomed appetite.

Then of a sudden all is changed. Of a sudden
the polite world rings with the love of this dead
interloper for the Count's wife; and the Count's
position, through no fault of his, becomes one of
delicacy. I do not think that Count Bertrand, howsoever staunch a patron of the Gay Science, got
much pleasure out of your great song, Seignior,

To Geoffrey Rudel

that *Irat et dolent* which the spruce troubadours were singing everywhere about your devotion to the Count's wife. I doubt if he admired your big porphyry tomb as the Countess designed it, and as he paid for it; or if he praised very heartily those verses which his wife wrote as your epitaph. And when Dame Mélisande, after so many shared years of prosaic ups-and-downs, left him and the six children, in order that she might devote her life to grieving over Geoffrey Rudel, I can but hope that Count Bertrand spoke his mind freely, and married somebody else with insulting promptness.

For it was he who became the true victim of your heart-hunger for *la princesse lointaine*, through the fact that to him she had been accessible. It was he whom domnei smote vitally.

Now of that high form of love, called domnei, which in its nature was religious rather than sensuous, much has been written in another place. Domnei assumed that a virtuous and intelligent and mature gentlewoman was Heaven's most splendid creation in the physical world. She was most near to Heaven, and she revealed clearliest Heaven's powers, of all living beings. It followed that one's chosen lady was worshipped, at a respectful distance, as a divine symbol. She represented as much of God as might in this life be comprehended by human faculties: and to approach her with any carnal thoughts, such as one might entertain toward lesser women, and execute freely for one's body's comfort, was an unthought-of sacrilege.

"For he really knows nothing whatever about domnei"—says a troubadour somewhat senior to Geoffrey Rudel—"who desires possession of his lady. The love which turns into reality, ceasing to be a matter of pure worship, is no better than marriage. It is needed for a lover but to obtain rings and ribbons from his lady to make him the equal to the King of Castile. If he receives jewels from her and, perhaps occasionally, a kiss, this is sufficient for love's eternal nutriment."

In brief, it was enough to behold her perfections; to adore them; and to make in their honor hymns. Such was domnei.

*

*   *

Now I, for one, I can detect no flaw in the logic of these mediæval amorists, as mere logic. That a virtuous and intelligent and mature gentlewoman is indeed Heaven's masterpiece in the way of zoölogy, I regard as at any rate a tenable hypothesis; and granting it, all the rest follows naturally enough. The trouble is that, being human, these amorists perforce practised their logic during the course of human living, wherein logic seems always to be more or less out of place, and results in discomfort and unreason.

The worshipped lady, for instance, was necessarily, in an era when girl children of gentle birth went straight from the nursery to the bridal chamber, already married to some other gentleman of repute and high standing. The husband, who during his bachelorhood had been the servitor *par amours* of some other nobleman's wife, had no least right to be jealous of his own wife's lover: and, in fact, husbands did hardly ever give way to jealousy, so large is the power of convention.

Exceptions, of course, occurred: but they were frowned on. When, for example, by the husband of his lady in domnei, the famous troubadour Guillaume de Cabestaing was murdered, and his broiled heart was served up to her at dinner, it was generally felt that the laws of good breeding had been violated. A comminatory service, denouncing this excessive husband, the Baron of Castel-Roussillon, was promptly conducted at all Courts of Love. None the less, as to what emotions other than crude jealousy those twelfth-century husbands of the upper classes fell a prey, one speculates perforce.

*

*   *

For almost always, be it remembered, the husband was an ageing poet. It is not possible for us nowadays, Seignior, to imagine a society in which every gentleman was (at least in his intentions) a poet: and yet in your day such was the case. The husband of every noble lady whom this or the other troubadour traversed Europe adoring, at the very top of his voice, was himself a retired poet, with all the high-pitched youth of a poet no great way behind him. And Count Bertrand, some twenty years earlier, as it happens, had been a mildly notable troubadour, in the days when he served *par amours* the Lady Adelais des Baux, and

148

wrote those lofty observations as to domnei and the King of Castile and so on which I quoted a little while since.

So when Count Bertrand heard your songs in praise of his wife, those songs of a strain so much loftier than his modest talents had ever touched, and when he saw you die very cheerily for the fond privilege of kissing her hand—the hand of that now and then exasperating, if good-hearted, and certainly in no way extraordinary woman who snored at Count Bertrand's side every night,— then he remembered, I imagine, his own youth. He recalled, I suspect, a time when he too had been just as idiotic: and after thinking a bit ruefully about that once lovely and all-perfect Adelais —she who was a gray quiet grandmother now, far oversea in Provence, and for whom he no longer cared a snap of his gouty fingers,—why, then, I fancy, even Count Bertrand envied you your death, Seignior, at the high tide of your youth and of your insane infatuation.

Given but the quarter of an hour's private conversation with you, he could, the Count knew, have cured your adoring, simply by telling you the exact truth about your lady in domnei, in respect to those points where a husband's knowledge is extensive and peculiar. Yet, the Count knew also, he could never have done it. For he too, Seignior, had once been a poet. He too, in his faraway youth, had served faithfully his lady in domnei.

*

*   *

And pardie! Count Bertrand reflected, out of the dead years she still looks at us oldsters now and then, that lady in domnei. Her face is pensive, and it appears half reproachful, somehow; but her face is more beautiful than are the faces of to-day's pink-and-white twitterers. Her like does not any longer exist. And ohimé! with an odd pang of adoration, we old fellows comprehend that she too did not ever exist, except in the wild fancies of a boy, who does not exist either, nowadays . . . Yes, it all seems very remote and futile and strangely dear. For I was a poet once; and I suffered hellishly because of it; and I do not want any of that nonsense back. Flayed men, these poets: a touch agonizes them. So they babble their idiocy,

To Geoffrey Rudel

about rings and ribbons and the King of Castile.
That is thin fare for one yet able, thanks be to St.
Foutin, to run his three courses amorously . . .
No, I do not want Adelais back, not even with renewed youth for both of us. Mélisande suits me
far better: she knows a man's ways, his taste in
food, his need of an extra-legal piece of tail now
and then, and his not meaning all that he says
when matters go wrong, and, in short, she under-
stands me—more or less. So we get on well enough
. . . Now Adelais was impractical. I could never
have lived up to her eternal sugared sermons
about sobriety and honor and continence and high
art and self-denial and a man's religious duties
and all those other superb notions of hers. It was
a relief to be rid of her, in a way: I stayed drunk
for a month, with nobody nagging at me like a
distressed angel. No doubt she assumed a great
deal of that high-mindedness for my benefit. I do
not recall she applied any such notions to her old
rip of a husband and his two catamites. To the
contrary, they all four got on well enough . . .
But I, I believed her each word adoringly. I was
then just such a young fool as this Rudel. And if
I had died then, I would have died a more splen-

did creature than I now am, or have any least desire to be. I would have died believing in every
one of those superb notions. Cry haro! for I instead have lived long enough to perceive that these
notions are not applicable to the life of a gentleman in this world, who has his estates to look after,
and his infidel neighbors to look after, and his
rheumatism also. In brief, I envy this young Rudel
because he died utterly a fool . . . God rest his
fine, clean callow soul! say I: for of such, my chap-
lain assures me, is the kingdom of Heaven.

Thus far one can well imagine Count Bertrand
to have meditated, somewhat as the ageing knights
thought about Galahad, in the half-remorseful
fashion with which an old poet regards the emotions of very young people, and half wishes that
he could accept them seriously.

*

*   *

Of course when his Mélisande left him, to enter
a nunnery, the affair took on a different complexion. An elderly gentleman, howsoever poeti-

cally inclined, does not care to have his household disrupted and his little domestic comforts upset in this wholesale fashion. But up to the day of her evasion, I fancy, Count Bertrand sneakingly sympathized with you, Seignior, somewhat to the above effect: and for my part, I sympathize with Count Bertrand entirely.

For you in the outcome there was paradise; the Countess had the ever-present solace of religion and the blessed assurance of rejoining you by-and-by, Seignior, in an eternal union: but for Count Bertrand there was merely the problem of raising six children unaided. Let none doubt that his second wife had a plain face and the most prosaic disposition in all Syria.

THE ELEVENTH LETTER:

To Lord Timur the Splendid

"Now Heaven not twice hath made a conqueror
So famous as is mighty Tamburlaine."

THE ELEVENTH LETTER:

To Lord Timur the Splendid

Greetings, Highness, as I must call you simply, inasmuch as it was your proud whim to be neither king nor emperor in a world over abundant with such commonplace potentates. You remained merely Amir Timur Gurigan—Lord Timur the Splendid—to whom all monarchs within travelling distance were your subjects. And you travelled a great deal. Born the son of a private country gentleman, an inferior sheep-herding chieftain of the Barlas Tatars, you overran, and you became absolute ruler of, every country between Greece and China.

You were master, in brief, of all India, of Persia and Media, of Arabia, and of the land of Kharesm;

of Erzerum, of Armenia the Less, and of Tabriz also. You reigned over such pleasingly entitled places as the Land of Silk, and the City of the Sultan, and the Land of the Sun. You were overlord likewise of the Land of Shadows. The Kurds and the Mongols served Lord Timur, as did several dozens of yet other nations. You besieged, and you destroyed, Damascus: you took by storm both Bagdad and Babylon, those ineffable old fortresses of romance. You defeated in open battle the Great Turk, Bajazet, who was called the Thunder, then the most powerful emperor on this planet: you kept him afterward in an iron cage which was very handsomely gilded, treating him always with unfailing courtesy . . . You managed, in short, during the latter half of the fourteenth century, somehow to escape from the more gorgeous books of Lord Dunsany into our flesh-and-blood world.

So did you live and prosper, quite incredibly; and develop into a shrivelled, partially blind, nearly toothless, infirm, crippled, quiet, stout-hearted little old gentleman, who still rode continuously about Asia, huddled up on the back of a white stallion, winning battles half absent-mindedly. It had be-

To Timur the Splendid

come with you an obsession "to achieve glory and
to found your dynasty." Each one of your sons was
a king nowadays; but of your grandsons, as they
came of age, you made emperors. With all these
parvenu monarchs you were fondly indulgent,
fretting only when they unfilially beat you at chess,
a game which you delighted in and played very
badly. You stayed always the most mild-mannered
of mortal beings in every private relation: to your
courtiers and to your generals you were as a supreme, and genial, and a drowsily ageing god, to
whom the enlightened would render loving service
and lose as many chess games as seemed humanly
possible.

To your adversaries likewise you remained constantly gracious, allowing every besieged city two
entire days in which to surrender and to become
your property without further oppression. But
upon the third day—for it sometimes happened
that the adversaries of Lord Timur proved regrettably obstinate—your drums sounded and your
scarlet banners were lowered. Thereafter your
armies advanced under black banners, as a token
that no one inhabitant of that city would be spared;
and in due course the men and the women and the

children of that city were faithfully butchered. No city and no kingdom, throughout the length of some forty years, had withstood successfully the assaults of the former sheep-tender.

All the while you remained, I repeat, merely Lord Timur. In your public documents, with it may be a misguided sense of humor, you described yourself as "I, Timur, servant of God." But your enemies jeeringly called you Timur-i-lang, or Timur the Limper, on account of your lameness in one foot, as the result of an arrow wound received during battle, very shortly after Amir Timur Gurigan had quitted his sheep cotes for conquests.

*

*   *

In Europe your military exploits were profoundly admired, the more so, of course, because of their reassuring remoteness. The Greek Emperor Manuel, as being too near a neighbor to neglect the amenities, sent frequent gifts to Lord Timur. He thus maintained with you a polite cor-

To Timur the Splendid

respondence, as did King Charles the Sixth of France and King Henry the Fourth of England: the King of Castile in due form despatched to your court an ambassador. First this ambassador, then the Byzantine chroniclers, and a bit later the Italians (including a Pope), began to publish biographies of Lord Timur; in this way did the events of your life and the more gaudy glories of your incredible dominion become known throughout Europe.

Even after you had been buried at Samarkand, in the year 1405, under a domed tomb roofed with turquoises, did the historians continue to write about this unbelievable Timur-i-lang, whom most of them called Tamburlaine . . . But you were no longer actively dreadful, no longer "news," no longer an object of perturbed interest to kings and large nations. Only scholars nowadays concerned themselves about Timur-i-lang, in the quiet of their studies, very occasionally . . . Your biographies became more brief, shrinking into parentheses, into passing allusions, into footnotes . . . You were merely a name found in old books. Thus drearily dwindled away your glory . . . But, well-nigh two centuries after your death, in or about

Ladies and Gentlemen

the year 1587, young Christopher Marlowe, then just graduated from Corpus Christi College at Cambridge, completed the first part of his *Tamburlaine the Great*.

*

*   *

So did you, Highness, who in your day esteemed the fine arts and patronized polite letters politely, create an entire literature. For with this *Tamburlaine* began, to every intent, the long and varied progress of Elizabethan tragedy and the yet continuing progress of English blank verse. I do not know of any recorded monarch who bestowed, howsoever unpremeditatedly, upon a foreign nation a gift more splendid.

It is granted that, like King Hamlet, you would find in your saga not much of the familiar. Conceivably, you would even frown, here and there, over this so continuously rhapsodizing account of one "Who, from a Scythian Shepheard, by his rare and woonderfull Conquests, became a most puissant and mighty Monarque, and (for his tyranny and

162

To Timur the Splendid

terrour in Warre) was tearmed The Scourge of God." For this Marlowe has made you, Highness, throughout and above all else, a poet; and poets, as your Highness well knew through your casual patronage of them, do not conquer empires. Yes, quite conceivably, you would frown, here and there. Yet by so doing, you would attest that weakness in judgment to which the most great of men are subject upon occasions . . . Let none blame you. It is exceedingly difficult for you heroes to grant that every sort of mortal action is transient save only the proper putting together of the properly selected words; and that all human splendors must depend by-and-by on the charity of a weakling poet for their survival.

For what, Highness, what would become of you empire-builders were it not for these ineffectual poets? The declared intent of your life was "to achieve glory and to found your dynasty." And in both attempts you appeared, throughout the length of almost two centuries, to have failed. You had become merely a name found in old books, a name without any vivid connotations, when Marlowe saw fit to revive you. Only a few scholars, frowsting in their studies, thought about Timur-i-lang, one way or the other. Your great glory had crumbled into nothingness.

Your empire too crumbled, very promptly, after the decease of Lord Timur; it has quite vanished nowadays. All that endures physically of Lord Timur is his forlorn tomb, despoiled of its turquoise, pitted everywhere with Russian rifle bullets: only one of its arches remains standing. And the three aged mullahs, in torn purple robes and extremely soiled white turbans, who yet guard your tomb, when they were asked, by your very latest biographer, "Who was Lord Timur?" replied unconcernedly:

"We do not know. He lived a great while before our births, and before the births of our fathers. It was a long time ago."

But in other and more noisy lands, this Marlowe has gained for you, Highness, that everlasting glory which you desired; and which he might just as easily have flung, while sipping meditatively at his clary wine or his xeres wine, to Attila or to Genghis Khan. It is true that, in addition, he gave you a wife and children, and a vast number of acquaintances, of whom you had not heard previously, and that he ensured the entire splendor

164

To Timur the Splendid

of your doings by inventing a great many of them. Such are the undoubted inconveniences of your immortality: yet were it not for Christopher Marlowe, you would have enjoyed, in all likelihood, no immortality, nor any least meed of remembrance, of any kind. It is the odd knack of these poets that they, an infirm and unstable folk, are yet able to build up everlastingly, out of much perishable stuff, the repute of complete strangers, quite irresponsibly.

*

* *

Moreover, Highness, it appeared that you had failed in the attempt to establish a dynasty. You outlived, I believe, all but one of your sons; and the Timurids, your grandsons, proved an enfeebled tribe, of whom tuberculosis and drink and amorously talented women and insanity made undesirable endings. Nevertheless did this Marlowe give to you, very long after your death, your new and more glorious children, in place of Jahangir and Omar and Rukh—making of you, Tamburlaine,

unpredictably, the begetter alike of Titus Andron-
icus and Romeo and Othello, of Bosola and Ven-
dice and Sir Giles Overreach, and of all those
countless Giovannis and Lorenzos and Isabellas
and Hippolytas and Sebastians and Julias and An-
tonios with whom the lesser Jacobeans have in-
continently colonized the fictitious "Italy" wherein occur their most high and incredible tragedies.

No other monarch ever reared such a huge, or a
less commonplace, family. For directly descended
from you, in this or the other degree, is every one
of these explosively splendid persons "who spend
their lives in murder and in intrigue, dress up as
men if they are women, as women if they are men,
see ghosts, run mad, and die in the greatest profusion on the slightest provocation". . . You thus
did, after all, found your dynasty, in a race truly
superb, if not over easy to live with; and you left
a long line of descendants which thrived, at any
rate, down to and through the very last written
tragedy in blank verse by Swinburne.

So in your ruined tomb may you rest content,
Highness—you about whom during your lifetime
it was declared, truthfully, after all, by the scribe
Sherif ad-Din, "The Lord Timur is so gifted as

To Timur the Splendid

to succeed in every one of his enterprises." For you did succeed in your two major endeavors, even though your triumph occurred by pure chance, a long time after you, the All-Conqueror, the adored and the dreaded of humankind, had become rotten bones, and were some while past caring about either success or failure.

THE TWELFTH LETTER:

To Sir John Falstaff of Caister in Norfolk

"For anything I know, Falstaff shall die of a sweat, unless already a' be killed with your hard opinions; for . . . this is not the man."

THE TWELFTH LETTER:

To Sir John Falstaff of Caister in Norfolk

When you departed this life, Sir John—at your
country place, in Norfolk, in the November of
1459—none doubts that you died, as became a pre-
eminently religious English gentleman, in the hope
of a glorious resurrection. How very mercifully
was hid from you the too speedy fulfilment of
your aspirations! For you had looked to be revived by Dan Gabriel his dreadful and holy trum-
pet: in no wild fever dream could it by any chance
have occurred to you that a lewd heathen goddess,
the Muse of Comedy, would prove your awakener
—and to an apotheosis how incredible, how sordid,
how cruel, how delightful!

If I become exclamatory, Sir, it is because no

171

considerate person can regard the unfairness of your doom without giving a loose to some natural emotion. For eighty and more years you had lived with piety and intelligence and honor, with a clear conscience and your due of worldly success. You had been an admired soldier during at least thirty-five of these years. Throughout some two or three campaigns, indeed, you had commanded all the English expeditionary forces in the French wars, winning as generalissimo the great battle of the Herrings, in which you fought against the combined armies of Scotland and France; you had been governor of Maine and Anjou; you were a knight of the Garter; and toward the end of your life (in a castle which covered no less than six acres of Norfolkshire) you thrived notably as a retired capitalist, as an extensive land-holder, as an open-handed philanthropist, and as a judicious patron of learning.

You had been yelped at, of course, by the envious, like any other prospering person; and a charge of military blunders you were once forced to repel—with entire success. Yet the sole failings more or less plausibly imputed to you appear to have been a certain rigor in your business dealings,

To Sir John Falstaff

as an unlenient creditor, and something of fa-
naticism in the practice of your religion. You inclined, in brief, to be a bit of a Puritan a good
while before puritanism had been labelled. Such,
then, was the honored and austere gentleman who
died in the November of 1459, after thriftily sub-
sidizing "seven religious men" and "seven poor
folk" to pray perpetually for his soul's welfare;
and whom that bad baggage, Thalia, saw fit to revive prematurely, about a hundred and forty years
later.

It skills not, Sir John, to repeat through what
causes you were thrust up into a pillory originally
meant for your colleague in arms, Lord Cobham.
The point is that at this time, about 1599, a poet
gave you new life upon earth, at a price which to
a man of your known business principles, and of
your painstaking respectability, might well have
appeared exorbitant. Since with your other virtues
you combined a gentleman's share of scholarship
(as befitted a co-founder of St. Mary Magdalen
College) you will recall, no doubt, that of the
great Greek captain Achilles it is recorded how, in
Ades' dim realm, he declared to his former com-
rade, to wily Odysseus, that it was better to live

in earth's sunlight as a slave than to be king over the shadowy nations of the dead. But I question if even this feebly whining Achilles (upon whose heroic nature death seems to have acted rather deleteriously) would have been content to live again as the Sir John Falstaff whom the last three centuries have known and—it is the bitter truth, Sir—have laughed at.

*

*   *

For the poet who revived you, Sir John, has left you not one shielding rag of gentility. He has set you a-stagger among us, an obscene gross belching tun-belly, out at the elbows, reeking of sack, gray with iniquity. Of the skilled and triumphant soldier this poet has made a faintheart; of the Puritan, a wencher; of the magnate, a wastrel; and of the staid business man, a Dionysiac choregus of all riot, immortality's darling. He has made of you, in brief, a calumny so engaging to human fancy that by no chance will mankind ever give up this counterfeit Falstaff in order to accord you, Sir, the

174

To Sir John Falstaff

respect and the praise which, living, you earned amply. Your case is outrageous; no man was ever libelled with more striking injustice; but your case is hopeless.

It is at all times the privilege of the artist to recreate history; provided only he has genius, he can elude punishment and compel belief: but I know of no instance in which this birthright has been abused more wantonly than when Shakespeare gave to the future his caricature of Sir John Falstaff. For Thackeray, or for Dumas, or for Maurice Hewlett—to cite but three prevaricators among thousands—when they libelled severally the Old Chevalier, or Catherine de Medici, or Mary Stuart, there was at least the excuse that the story they had in hand moved on the hinges of calumny. The events of their victims' lives and the nature of their victims' characters have been somewhat misrepresented, for utilitarian ends, for the plot's sake; and at worst, the sin is an affair of recoloring and of shifted emphases. But you, Sir John, have been endowed with all the vices you shunned; stripped of the many virtues which you practised faithfully throughout eighty and some years; and thrust into miry actions with which you had no more to do than had Aretino or King Arthur. As a member of the Protestant Episcopal Church, I cannot doubt that the soul of William Shakespeare is eternally damned for his parody of a devout Christian gentleman: and I doubt not, either, that upon holidays and the major saints' days you are permitted to peep in at his torments. It is your full due.

*

*　　*

Yet, as a writer, I am conscious of some little sneaking complacency. Heaven made the flesh-and-blood Falstaff of the very best human material, turning out an exceptionally fine specimen of divine craftsmanship. By-and-by (through what exact causes we shall not ever know) a mere writer, the approved captain of my clan, made us another Falstaff after his own notions, a lewd and thoroughgoing and high-spirited libel, a gay trucidation of truth. And promptly the romance drove the reality out of the field of human beliefs. I educe a quaint moral which—to your somewhat puritanic

To Sir John Falstaff

ears, Sir John—it seems wiser not to express explicitly.

Yet do you take what lean comfort you may, Sir,
from knowing that this slanderer has defamed not
you alone . . . Indeed, one cannot but wonder
over this Shakespeare whensoever one considers his
never-failing absence of conscience in the presence
of history. Caution may pardonably have prompted
his maligning of King Richard the Third to a
certain extent, when the granddaughter of that
Tudor who stole England from the last Plantag-
enet still sat on the throne of England: but it does
seem to be carrying caution too far, to accredit
Richard with murdering virtually all members of
the upper classes who died, whether by disease or
due process of law or through any other cause,
during his brief life, in addition to a few who survived him . . . And again, mere time-serving may
have led Shakespeare to slander Macbeth in comparison with that Banquo who enjoyed the dubious honor of being the direct ancestor of King
James the First. Nevertheless did Shakespeare, who
had read his Holingshed's *Chronicles of Scotland*
(in the edition of 1587) very well know that Macbeth had a quite tenable claim to the Scots throne;

that he did not murder Duncan through treachery, but instead, with the assistance of Banquo, openly "slewe the king at Envernes, or, as some say, at Botgosuane"; and that afterward Macbeth reigned wisely and righteously for "XVII years over the Scottishmen," during which period "he accomplished many worthie actes right profitable to the common wealth." Such were the known and essential facts upon which the tragedy of *Macbeth* —to express matters as mildly as may be—does not dwell with untactful honesty.

Upon this playwright's wanton assassination of King Hamlet, that lordly Jutlander, in defiance of all history books, I have remarked in another place. Ah, but no less wickedly, Sir John, did this regicide deal with King Lear, fabling that the old gentleman died insane in a prison house, whereas in point of fact (as you will remember, Sir, who took a soldier's pride in your English history) stout Lear and his French army "fought with his enemies and reduced both his sons-in-law under his power"—thus winning back his England, and afterward reigning prosperously, even until he died of old age and was buried in the bed of a river. Before the Shakesperean version of Jeanne

To Sir John Falstaff

d'Arc (that same Pucelle against whom you fought
with misguided valor, Sir, and whose martyrdom
in Rouen's market-place you quite possibly wit-
nessed) one can but observe that, unless the Roman Catholic Church has been sadly misled, this
picture cannot well be the faithful likeness of a
properly canonized saint. But before the man's version of Julius Cæsar one retires, in mere silent
stupefaction.

*

*   *

I might cite you yet other instances, Sir John,
of this poet's idle and lewd lying as to his betters.
Let these few suffice to assure you of your many
and great comrades in misfortune, of your fellow
sufferers under the spew of his slanderings! And
yet, wit ye well, Sir John, I educe that nothing
whatever can be done about it. This little War-
wickshire calumnist had no conscience: that is
granted. But he had genius, against which no
other virtue may prevail.

I educe also, Sir John, that your own special and

your far more respectable virtues have gone un-
rewarded. I educe that, for once, the memory of the
just is not blessed. And I educe, in asking leave of
you, that the innate depravity of man's nature is
well attested by the fact that before your undeserved obloquy we stand charmed, and applaud the
outrage delightedly. For Heaven made you good
and great and successful: but art has made you
amusing.

THE THIRTEENTH LETTER:

To Dr. Johan Faustus of Kundling, of Cracow, and of Wittenberg

"I wonder what's become of Faustus, that was wont to make our schools ring with sic probo?"

THE THIRTEENTH LETTER:

To Dr. Johan Faustus of Kundling, of Cracow, and of Wittenberg

So fallen is your estate, Sir, that your main function nowadays is to keep people away from the opera. "It is only *Faust* to-night," they say. "Let's not go." And the person addressed will, as a rule, assent cheerfully enough, because—as a tenor rôle —you have become an unvalued antique, to the majority of us, a long while ago.

Tenors have not much in common with antiques, I admit, except that their legs are so rarely of the best period. And besides that, one does customarily feel, after the first act of *Faust*, that while Mephistopheles was about the task of rejuvenating you, he might better have made a complete job of it, by restricting your waistline and abdomen, which retain still the majestic contours of sedate middle life. In fact, Sir, inasmuch as Gounod has so arranged matters that in your love-affair you have no rival except a contralto most unconvincingly dressed as a boy, one admits that Marguerite is not blessed with the happiest possible choice of seducers . . . Yet does the facility with which she allows your entrance into her bedroom, within twenty-five minutes of your first meeting, rather strikingly justify her brother Valentine's admonition at parting, to let men alone during his absence. He knew more about Marguerite and about Marguerite's past than we do. For one, I have not ever quite felt she deserved the luxury of that uncommonly large and airy prison cell in the last act, in addition to a jailer so unsuspicious by nature as to accept her singing trios in the middle of the night as an affair of course. Most jailers would think this a phenomenon calling for prompt investigation.

—All which musical criticism has led me some distance from my point, that to most of us, Dr. Faustus, you have become merely the tenor rôle in an opera of which we have grown more or less tired.

To Dr. Johan Faustus

It seems an odd avatar for you who, living, termed yourself the demi-god of Heidelberg, *Philosophus Philosophorum*, the fountain of necromancers, astrologer, chiromancer, aëromancer, and pyromancer, in addition to yet other magniloquent titles; and by your contemporaries were described as a vagabond, an empty babbler, a mere fool, an infamous beast, a sodomite, and a cesspool of countless devils. But the truth about you, as about all of us, lies somewhere between a man's private notion of himself and the publicly expressed opinions of his neighbors as to the same topic.

*

*   *

We know that you were born, toward the end of the fifteenth century, at Kundling (which is now Knittlingen) in Württemburg; that you studied magic at Cracow in Poland; and that you by-and-by came to the newly-opened University of Wittenberg to take up, by a somewhat startling change, the study of divinity. You were not destined, however, to adorn the church. Instead (to every appearance,

185

Ladies and Gentlemen

in the year of grace 1515) you made your well-
known and supremely unclerical pact with Mephistopheles, whereby your soul was transferred to
this fiend in exchange for twenty-four years of his
services. Yet were you not incited to your bargain,
it so happened, by the sight of a soprano in a blond
wig, viewed through a strip of gauze. You were in-
flamed otherwise, by the scholar's more rarefied lust
to acquire knowledge and still more knowledge.
You desired to fathom, in one stinted human lifetime, all the secrets of heaven and earth, and of hell
also.

Now this is a fact as to which your first known
biographers would seem to compete with Gounod
in their ignorance. They write from the firm standpoint of a shocked church communicant, to whom
all dealings with a devil (no matter what may be
their purpose or who argues about them) remain
devilish. Your German biographer, in 1587, it may
interest you to know, was content to describe you,
Sir, on his title page, "as an awful and abominable
Example and sincere Warning to all presumptuous,
inquisitive and godless Persons." But the Englishman who in 1592 translated, or rather paraphrased,
this memoir goes its author one better. By his very

To Dr. Johan Faustus

title does he express his exact personal opinion of
you, through renaming his paraphrase, *The History
of the Damnable Life and Deserved Death of Dr.
John Faustus*. No mortal, after that, is likely to begin reading the book under any misleading impres-
sion that your biographer admires you to a pre-
Stracheyan extent.

Nevertheless does this book—without, to all ap-
pearances, its writer's ever suspecting the circumstance—make plain, and make plain over and yet
over again, the fact that you were driven hellward
by the scholar's desire to acquire knowledge and
still more knowledge. It is a quaint phenomenon: I
can parallel it only by Thackeray's obvious ignorance that his Mrs. Mackenzie, in *The Newcomes*,
was what we nowadays describe as a bathroom
drinker.

You wanted knowledge. You desired, as do most
of us, a sufficiency of fine food and sound wine and
fair women; and your taste in humor was both crude
and unbridled. But, for the most part, you made of
your wretched Mephistopheles, throughout twenty-
four years, an unresting combination of the school-
master, of the touring agency, and of the Queries
and Answers column in a newspaper. One rather

pities the poor devil; and suspects that, when the harsh term of his servitude was over, he retired to hell completely outworn. One is quite sure that he never again undertook the arduous task of damning a philosopher.

*

*   *

Meanwhile you acquired knowledge. You observed the cities and the customs of many men, making a grand tour of the planet in fifteen days, like an excessive Phineas Fogg, and yet later recombing the principal and most famous lands of the world, with particular attention to all public buildings which Baedeker, if granted this privilege thus early in earth's history, would most certainly have starred. The amenities of Paradise also you inspected, "from the least distance whence all men whosoever are denied to come any nearer." The Garden of Eden was lighted upon this occasion, for your special convenience, by "a mighty clear strike of fire coming from heaven." It is not recorded how Mephistopheles secured this supernal act of politeness. You

To Dr. Johan Faustus

visited hell also, with what appears rather morbid
haste. But, above all, you asked questions of Mephistopheles.

You asked him, for example, about Lucifer's first
fall and the events leading thereunto; about the
geography, the sub-divisions, and the governance,
of Lucifer's present kingdom; about how to interpret dreams; about predestination and pigeon
training; about the pains of the damned, the possibility of their final redemption, and the shape of
an archangel's sword. You inquired about the several planets, the cause of a lunar eclipse, and the
true nature of fire, air, water, and earth, and all
that which is contained in any one of them. You
asked of Mephistopheles the best formulæ for making oneself invisible, for mining precious stones, for
reviving Polyphemus, and for increasing one's
height. You asked also about the significance of
comets; about ghosts; about meteors, salamanders,
the hierarchy of heaven, the inner life of a monas-
tery, the proper brewing of ale, and how to cure
gout. You likewise required Mephistopheles to tell
you how to possess Helen of Troy, to remove superfluous hairs without shaving, to catch fish with your

189

hands, to read the lost comedies of Terence and
Plautus, to ride abroad on a beer barrel, to open
locked doors, and to cut off a man's leg without
giving him pain. You asked in the same breath for
an explanation of thunder and for a reliable method
to procure fresh fruits during the winter months.
And the poor devil, Sir, had to answer every one
of these questions at full length, and ever so many
yet other questions, just as your not-ever-sated curi-
osity prompted, for twenty-four years hand-running, or else tell you to go to heaven.

So then did you acquire knowledge ruthlessly,
until time released the tormented fiend from your
eternal question-asking. He wrung your neck forthwith, in the year 1539, at Staufen in the Breisgau;
dashed out your brains and your teeth; and flung
down your mangled corpse, from a third story
window, to a manure heap in the stable yard. One
does not defend such extremities; but, upon the
whole, one does understand them, provided that
devils possess any least share of human nature. In
fact, one rather admires the tenacity of Mephistopheles. No merely mortal being, no seraph, could
have put up with your eternal question-asking for
a whole twenty-four years . . . At all events, Sir,

To Dr. Johan Faustus

thus ended your ambitions, your curiosities, your learned delights, and your quest of universal knowledge—in a manure heap.

＊

＊   ＊

Well, and Marlowe fished you out of it, very much as he disinterred Lord Timur from his turquoise-roofed tomb, without ever fathoming your true nature. As of Timur, so of you, Christopher Marlowe made a poet. He assumed, as a plain matter of course, that a philosopher's main interests must be vested in poetry and in Helen of Troy and in riotous living and in yet other unphilosophical exercises. He imagined that you desired mere supernatural powers and mere superhuman indulgences, thrusting into a mouth adapted only to question-asking a vast number of unprovable, if highly poetic, direct statements. It would never have occurred to you, for instance, to declare, "A sound magician is a demi-god,"—not to you, who looked upon magic more practically, as a postgraduate course in one's education. And if ever you, Sir, had thought to inquire, "Was this the face that launched a thousand ships?"

191

you would have gone on immediately to ask about their names, captains, commissariat arrangements, and tonnage.

Goethe, himself a bit of a pedant, understood you far better. Goethe quite clearly saw that you wanted to fathom, in one stinted human lifetime, all the secrets of heaven and earth, and of hell also . . . But, alas, Sir, it was Goethe who first involved you with that Margaret whom Gounod a while later gallicized into Marguerite, with the attendant necessity of making you a tenor who can sing the *"Salut demeure"* acceptably.

*

*   *

"What has Margaret to do with Faust?" asked Charles Lamb: and I do not think anybody has ever answered him. For one, I simply cannot imagine your perturbed embarrassment, Dr. Faustus, were you to learn that the world at large now remembers you as an elderly nincompoop who gave up his soul's salvation in order to seduce an underbred working-girl. It is not to be denied, in view of your

192

To Dr. Johan Faustus

sextuple achievements in the Sultan of Turkey's seraglio, that upon occasion you could distinguish yourself as a loose liver: but all such affairs were mere *hors-d'œuvres* in a continuous orgy of knowledge-guzzling. For at bottom you wanted only, let it be repeated, knowledge. So you got knowledge, at the one possible if somewhat stiff price; and having got it, you carried off your unparalleled knowledge triumphantly, even to your manure heap. It was permitted you to reflect, in the same instant that Mephistopheles was dashing out your brains, that these were the best-stocked brains ever exercised by a descendant of Adam. You had found out the exact truth as to everything touching mortal life, including now the quaint pangs of its dissolution.

So did you obtain to as happy an outcome for any human endeavor as a philosopher could reasonably expect. But that he, the philosopher himself, should be made, willy-nilly, and without so much as a voice test, the tenor in an out-of-date opera, Sir, seems an affliction well beyond reason, an unprophesiable ill. It is likewise an affliction for which not any recognized school of philosophy—in so far as I now recall—has prescribed any recognized cure.

THE FOURTEENTH LETTER:

To the Lady Rebecca Rolfe, Called
Pocahontas

"But you, O you,
   So perfect and so peerless, are created
   Of every creature's best."

THE FOURTEENTH LETTER:

To the Lady Rebecca Rolfe, Called Pocahontas

Whost I reflect, Madame, that you quitted this
mortal life as lately as 1617, leaving issue only one
infant son, then am I puzzled by the number of your
grandchildren, in varying generations, to-day living. It does not seem possible that such hordes of
Southerners should be descended from you as to
make any Virginian who cannot boast of this honor,
in at least one lineage, feel somewhat conspicuous.

To that conspicuousness I perforce admit—and
yet it is with a qualification. Even though, through
some inexplicable falling out of events, I did happen
to be born in Virginia without thus becoming your
grandchild, I may at any rate declare myself to be
your cousin, inasmuch as I convey about earth some

197

portion of the blood of Opechancanough, your uncle . . . Him, it appears probable, you have not forgotten. No person who encountered Opechancanough seems ever to have forgotten, while life lasted, that dark statesman who was so far in advance of his era that, as early as 1622, he foresaw the necessity of restricting immigration into this country. Since this was after your death, Madame, I must tell you that upon this occasion he diminished the Colony of Virginia through the rough and ready methods of a massacre: and even though (on account of a regrettable forewarning conveyed to the English, by one of his followers) he succeeded in killing off only three hundred and forty-seven of the pale-face settlers, out of a total of twelve hundred and fifty-eight, that was nevertheless, I submit, a highly creditable score, such as we have not since equalled. Neither during the Revolution nor the War of 1812 did the defenders of our country manage to despatch one out of every four of the invading English.

Do you not mistake me, Madame! It is not my object in this place to vaunt the patriotic services of my ancestor, your revered uncle. I wish only to make plain that kinship which exists between us,

To Pocahontas

before speaking with the frankness which kinship ordinarily warrants and not infrequently abuses. And, with our cousinhood thus established, I desire to address you as to your legend—that very fine legend about which so much excellent nonsense has been published by a large host of Americans and by at any rate two Englishmen.

For, as I pointed out some little time ago, Madame my cousin, in commenting upon a book which Mr. David Garnett has written about your picturesque legend, Mr. Garnett is not the first and one Englishman to be beguiled by the august Emperor Powhatan's best-known daughter. As all good Thackerayans will remember, Mr. George Esmond Warrington also (shortly after his runaway marriage with Miss Theo Lambert, and no great while after his well-merited theatrical success with the play *Carpezan*) attempted a tragedy upon Pocahontas. Such Thackerayans will recall likewise that, at its opening and only performance, at Drury Lane Theatre, with the bewitching Pritchard in the title rôle, Mr. Warrington's *Pocahontas* failed flatly— here one quotes the playwright's own rueful admission—on account of its "actual *fidelity to history*."

I have noted in this fashion these facts because of

an American's natural delight whensoever any Englishman condescends to write a book about America; and because, in the second place, Mr. Garnett
has aped Mr. Warrington not merely in theme but
in historical excess also, to an extent which seems to
me to make Mr. Garnett's book unexhilarating
reading; and because, in the third place, I really do
wonder why the involved bit of our family's history,
Madame my cousin, should have been thought
worthy of such careful adhesion, by either author.

*

* *

For you, Madame, have been made, through no
apparent fault of yours, if not the first, at least the
first feminine member, of that edifying line of humbugs which keep salutary, and which render ever
popular, the approved history of a republic peculiarly partial to humbugs. All the great-grandchil-
dren of Macaulay's every schoolboy know the
circumstances of your heroic rescue of Captain John
Smith from the bludgeons of your father Powhatan.
And that is quite as it should be, inasmuch as, upon

To Pocahontas

this ever-memorable occasion, your conduct was of
a cast so noble as to evoke one's honest regret that
you should never have heard of it,—any more, of
course, than did Columbus ever hear about the dis-
covery of America, or George Washington about
his cherry-tree, or Barbara Frietchie about her flag
waving.

I speak in confidence; and indeed, as becomes a
Virginian, I speak with extreme reluctance. Not
openly, of my own will, would I impugn a legend
so highly esteemed by my fellow taxpayers. Nevertheless am I forced in my private thoughts to grant
that all which we know about your legend, Madame,
is what that mundivagant soldier, Captain John
Smith, is pleased to tell us: and, as was well ruled
by the late Justice Stareleigh, in *Bardell vs. Pick-
wick*, what the soldier said is not evidence.

For, alas, Madame, so strangely contagious is
the force of an ill example that I too, in approach-
ing your legend, cannot refrain from a little "actual
fidelity to history." It is, I mean, an awkward but
an historical fact, that in Smith's first account of his
Virginian adventures, as it was published in 1608,
immediately after his capture by the Pamunkey In-
dians, he says nothing in particular about you,

beyond complimenting, with a few polite commonplaces, your "wit and spirit." Nor in this book does
he anywhere suggest any special need of a rescue
from your good father Powhatan, who figures in
the *True Relation* as a model of hospitality and
kindness.

Only when Smith's *General History of Virginia,
New England, and the Summer Islands* was printed,
a good fifteen years later—some little while after
you, as "the daughter of the Emperor of Virginia,"
had appeared at the court of James the First, and
had grown to be in England a much-talked-about
person—and when, above all, you were safely dead,
—then only, Madame, does Smith's knowledge of
your early life become clear and copious. Then only
does the Emperor Powhatan emerge, from a relatively uninteresting level of benevolence, as a fee-
foh-fum tyrant; then only does Pocahontas develop
into the patron saint of Captain John Smith especially and of the Virginian colony in general; and
then only, for the first time, does anybody hear
about your rescue of Captain John Smith in 1607,
a rescue which, to every appearance, had escaped
Smith's attention until 1623.

Even in Virginia, I reflect morbidly, the contradiction should have weight. (It has, of course, none whatever, in a state superior to logic.) Yet I, for one, I find need to reflect, howsoever privately, that at this exact time you, Madame, chanced to be excellent "copy"; that Smith was a hard-up publicist, a tried gambler at the conscienceless game; and that no person then living in England could dispute whatever he might say about either you or your imperial father, as concerned your actions some fifteen years earlier. I reflect, I repeat, upon these three stubborn and unarguable facts. And I educe from them (howsoever unwillingly) that to believe what Smith tell us, in the *General History*, as to you and the Emperor Powhatan necessitates the forgetting of a great deal about human nature and virtually everything which is known about Smith. I infer, in brief, that your entire legend is pure balderdash.

—But very excellent balderdash. This Smith, if not actually a great creative artist, was, in his rough way, a skilled adapter; and even though he made public the Pocahontas myth lyingly, for sheer money's sake, yet is it the right of every artist to be judged by his work rather than by his methods or motives. It was a most happy inspiration to repro-

duce and re-edit the flesh-and-blood Virginian
princess who had lately died in England, as the
Pocahontas who survives thrivingly in legend. Such
labors are necessary so that for every land may be
created its own special mythology and its pious
faith, suited to patriotic use upon national an-
niversaries, in its mighty and all-wise and sacred
forebears. Our land was just then evolving this
mythology: it had, as yet, no forebears: and its
pantheon stayed vacant except for an explorer or
so, who of necessity were mere foreigners. In the
true nick of time did Captain Smith have his fine
inspiration, at what we have since learned to describe as a well-chosen moment; and because of his
aptness, Madame, you became the first native-born
American to be enshrined in our land's mythology,
with or without what justice it does not in the least
matter nowadays.

*

*   *

The Pocahontas of your legend has, in any event,
an origin immeasurably antedating the year of grace

To Pocahontas

1607. She was known, I have not a doubt, in the first fireside tales of Egypt and China and Sumeria. It occurs to me, simply because I happened last month to re-read some of the *Kathasaritságara*, that in India she appears very early, at any rate twice, in the story of Sringabhuja, and again in the story of Chandasena.

I daresay that investigation, and a sad waste of time, would reveal her presence somewhere in *The Thousand and One Nights*. I do not know, because it has been a considerable while since I opened that verbose anthology. Turning toward fields familiar to everybody, however, it is certain that, as Medea and Ariadne and so on, she was familiar to Greek romanticists, this foreign princess who in her own foreign country shields the exploring, or it may be the shipwrecked, Greek hero from the enmity of her father; and who aids him to perform a task in her father's service; and who ultimately marries the hero. That was a dénouement from which Captain John Smith, when he came to write his own version of the old story, was debarred by the awkward fact that you had demonstrably married somebody else; yet did he evade his difficulty handsomely enough, by recording that you had married John Rolfe as a mere *pis aller*, in the belief that John Smith was dead.

It follows in plain justice, Madame, that your legend well merits its place in the folk-lore of America, inasmuch as it adorns the folk-lore of every other known nation. In this legend everywhere you remain pure and tender and wise and beautiful. Your father varies a deal more widely: he appears at odd times as a sultan, as a wood spirit, as a giant, as a magician, as an ogre, and very often as a demon on leave of absence from this or the other hades. In malevolence alone does he stay constant: like Powhatan, in Captain Smith's romance, he is always "more like a devil than a man." And always you, Madame, manage at the last pinch to save your lover, and to effect a compromise whereby, in place of dying, he performs for your father some task or service. Always, in brief, "Pocahontas, the King's dearest daughter, gets his head in her arms, and lays her own upon his, to save him from death: whereat the Emperor is contented he should live to make for him hatchets, and for her bells, beads, and copper." To make hatchets and beads is a considerable descent from the conquest of fire-breathing bulls

To Pocahontas

and the slaying of a Minotaur; but on his own scale Smith does not wander by one hair's breadth from the time-approved formula.

Ethnologists tell us that the old story is all a reminiscence of the yet older custom of marriage by purchase or by capture, which made the father the natural foe of the lover, either in bargain driving or in open battle. That is as it may be. Into their own troublous and cloudy realm of theorizing and of disputation and of innumerous, mostly incomprehensible, and by ordinary very long footnotes, I decline to follow these ethnologists.

*

*   *

For I do not think that Smith got you from folklore, except indirectly. It is more pleasure-giving to fancy his pilfering you from a source more august. Yes, it is cordially tempting to imagine that John Smith borrowed his idyllic revision of Pocahontas (when the gray vagabond came to rewrite your story) from none less than Shakespeare. When Smith reconstructed his account of you, in his *Gen-*

*eral History of Virginia, New England, and the
Summer Islands,* then *The Tempest* was still a new
and most popular play, based upon the late ship-
wreck of Sir George Somer's company in these same
"Summer Islands." Smith could not possibly have
ignored this famous comedy, inasmuch as Prospero's
"desert isle," howsoever indefinite its location otherwise, was quite definitely allied with Smith's subject matter. To any Jacobean audience—and it may
be, to Shakespeare too—this island was a part of
those magical Americas which Englishmen were at
the instant exploring.

Contemporary audiences, in brief, thought about
Miranda and Prospero as living somewhere in the
general neighborhood of that Virginia from which
"the Lady Rebecca" had lately come into England
to be a nine days' wonder. So one does unavoidably
speculate if, when Smith began to romance about
the Virginian princess and her father, he did not
borrow, from this popular notion, large hints as
to his revised version of Pocahontas and Powhatan?
Himself of course, as invariably his own hero, he
cast in the rôle of Prince Ferdinand, released from
fetching in logs of firewood, and set to making bells,
hatchets and beads . . . For here again, in *The*

To Pocahontas

Tempest, is the old story—the magician father resident in a foreign land, with a beautiful and tender-hearted daughter who shields the shipwrecked hero from enmity; who aids him to perform a task in her father's service; and who ultimately marries the hero.

I would not press this suggestion, beyond saying that in Shakesperean criticism I have encountered a great many hypotheses which seemed to me by an infinite deal wilder. And it is heart-warming to imagine that, with an honesty unusual among our foreign debtors, the Miranda whom Shakespeare borrowed from America has been duly returned to her native mythology, in the form of Pocahontas.

THE FIFTEENTH LETTER:

To Richard Cabell of Buckfastleigh, Devon, Armiger, Lord of the Manor of Brooke

"And now, my dear Watson, without referring to my notes I cannot give you a more detailed account of this curious case."

THE FIFTEENTH LETTER:

To Richard Cabell of Buckfastleigh, Devon, Armiger, Lord of the Manor of Brooke

It must remain to me always, Sir Richard, a source of regret that by another writer you were high-handedly plucked from my family-tree some while before I myself had the chance to employ you. For I still regard covetously your story. And I think too (such being the nature of every author) that he who borrowed your story might well have made something more of it.

Born in 1620, you were duly graduated from Balliol College and the Middle Temple, in order that, but a little later, you might graduate also in what uninformed persons speak of loosely as Black Magic. Yours was—by daylight—the leisured life of a country gentleman; you were an efficient justice of the

213

peace, a sedulous vestryman, an unfriend of poachers; and for at least three terms you served as Lord High Sheriff of Devonshire. Robert Herrick was your close associate: you had interests in common, even though the vicar of Dean Prior was in politics a Royalist. Throughout the Parliamentary Wars you yourself sided, as did most of the county, with Cromwell and his Puritans. People said that after dark your pursuits were not wholly puritanic.

People said, in brief, that your faith was the faith of Old Believers; and that the relations between Devonshire's officially recognized Jehovah and the obscure god whom you honored after nightfall stayed unfriendly.

At all events, when your bond had run out—in the October of 1677—then black hounds came racing over Dartmoor; and toward midnight they gathered around Brooke Manor House, breathing smoke and fire, and howling expectantly. These creatures, having served you for the agreed time, were come now for their agreed payment, the country-side remarked later. And these fire-breathing hounds obtained their earned wages: for at midnight you mounted your black mare, and you rode away, across the dark moor, in the company of these

To Sir Richard Cabell

hounds. Your body, when men found it, was badly
mangled; it was scorched here and there; and your
throat was torn open.

*

*   *

Well, Sir, and afterward—a long while afterward, in the year of grace 1902—one Dr. A. Conan
Doyle took over your story, renaming you Hugo
Baskerville. He reduced the company of your familiars to a single beast; and he lugged into your
story a superfluous "yeoman's daughter." After
that, he endowed you with a fictitious lot of brand-
new descendants, including none of our surname;
and he fetched down to Dartmoor the accomplished
Mr. Sherlock Holmes, accompanied by the amiable
Dr. Watson, to solve the problems you had be-
queathed these descendants. Doyle wrote, in brief,
with you as his point of departure, *The Hound of
the Baskervilles;* and he made out of your legend a
striking book.

But that is hardly the point. We all know how
Dr. James Mortimer, M. R. C. S., came (with his
silver-banded walking stick) to the lodgings in

Baker Street, and narrated your story. "I tell you, Watson, this time we have got a foeman who is worthy of our steel," said Sherlock Holmes, by-and-by; and went secretly into Devonshire, to deal with the Baskervilles, the Barrymores, and the Stapletons, throughout "some weeks of severe work." And it all ended happily enough, in a little dinner at Marcini's and a box at Covent Garden to hear the De Reszkes in *Les Huguenots* . . . Meanwhile my point is that Dr. Conan Doyle (who later became a knight and your peer) left out of his book that which is, to me, the most interesting part of your story.

＊

＊　　＊

For they record, Sir, that after your burial you did not rest quietly in your grave. Out of consideration for our family's feelings, I shall not rehearse in this place any details of the old and unpleasant sequel. It appears enough to say that your corpse was dug up and reburied in the same place, just outside the south porch of the parish church, with all

To Sir Richard Cabell

the ceremonies necessitated by your post-mortem
restlessness. And besides that, a very special edifice
was erected above your grave, to prevent your coming out again to trouble the neighborhood you had
once adorned.

This tomb, in so far as I remember it, is shaped
rather like a Chinese pagoda, with a weather vane,
taken from your manor house, a bit incongruously
fixed at the top of it . . . Should the dead, I meditated, heed whether the winds of earth move toward
this or the other pole? for wherein may it profit the
dead whether Boreas or bland Auster prevails? In
short, I had never seen any other tomb thus ornamented: and echo answered me nothing.

At all events, The Sepulchre, as Buckfastleigh
calls your last prison house, is kept locked: but the
more reckless of humankind are permitted to insert
their fore-fingers into the empty, large keyhole.
When anybody presumes to do this, you promptly
bite the intrusive finger: for inside your tomb, but
once more out of your grave, you remain active and
malevolent and very, very, very hungry. Luckily,
you cannot get out of The Sepulchre, without special aid—or so, at least, they told me at Buckfast-

leigh—because you were properly exorcised at the time of your second burial, with the harsh ritual appointed for vampires.

*

*   *

Now by the yet living members of your family in general you are regarded, I must tell you, Sir Richard, as a regrettable relative. (Herein your position is not unique: we have many such.) Yes, I have noted among your kinsmen a distinct tendency, in discussing their former glories, to slur over the third Sir Richard, in order to discuss such of those ancestors as were governors or burgesses or ministers of the gospel or aldermen, or yet something else more or less superior, from gentility's standpoint, to a mere vampire. In fine, I have observed a fixed if a tacit resolution to ignore you, Sir, as being still potentially alive, and as awaiting only to have the door of your pagoda-like sepulchre unclosed, in order that you may re-enter hungrily the orbit of human life.

Yet does this attitude toward you in some sort

To Sir Richard Cabell

appear unreasonable. For we of Virginia take a proper interest in our ancestors: I have heard that we even boast of them. Well, and in you, Sir, your kinsmen have an ancestor whom, by all reports, it is still possible to meet face to face. Of their many ancestors you alone remain immediately accessible: and yet not one single member of your family, during the last two hundred and fifty years, has attempted to arrange a conference. I alone of the race, I believe, have gone so far as even to put a finger inside your keyhole: and when you bit me, I too, let it be admitted, withdrew from Buckfastleigh churchyard without following up the acquaintance which you appeared rather avidly eager to make far more intimate.

I do not defend my conduct. It was prompted merely by prudence. From any rational standpoint, I admit that, as a kinsman, you ought not to have been thus coldly ignored, for your place in your family's pedigree is, or at any rate it ought to be, inalienable.

Yet at this point it occurs to me that, in the remote years when I was a genealogist, I often wondered over the events and the persons that all our older Virginian pedigrees do ignore. I refer not

merely to legends, not only to such dubious kinsmen as vampires. I am thinking about attested happenings which remain written down, and sworn to
by their witnesses, in our nominally public records
—to those peculiarly frank depositions which have
never been so much as hinted at in print.

We encounter here, I believe, a by-product of
feminism. All these historiettes are thus censored
—it is my firm theory—because they involve persons who are to-day the prized ancestors of the
badged, the large-bosomed, and the generally in-
timidating gentlewomen who hold office in patriotic
organizations. Bold men there be who may go
a-nesting in the eagle's eyrie, or who in the un-
pathed jungle may dare to rob the tigress of her
one cub; but what insane desperado anywhere
would dare rob the Colonial Dame, or the Daughter
of 1812, of her ancestor's good repute—except, at
utmost, in a disguised handwriting, through the
vehicle of an anonymous letter? So far as that goes,
I doubt if any veteran of the American Revolution,
no matter with what vigor he may have charged at
Bunker Hill or run away at Camden, could pluck
up the spirit to face his own descendants when they
have duly assembled, next April, at Washington,

To Sir Richard Cabell

in an embattled convention of the Daughters of the American Revolution. And why, I wonder, why, in high Heaven's name, is organized patriotism so very ruinous alike to the disposition, the candor, and the figure, of most women? . . . But I divagate. And admitting my errancy, I return forthwith to you, Sir Richard, with all humble apologies.

*

*   *

Well, Sir, your infernal dealings are but a matter of semi-private record, spoken of, at utmost, in such obscure publications as *The Cornwall and Devon Notes and Queries* (Volume 17) and in similar byways of the antiquary. Throughout the account rendered of you in the official book relative to your clan—*The Cabells and Their Kin*—there is, I must tell you, not any mention of your hounds, no whiff of sulphur, nor even one breath of scandal. For such, Sir Richard, is our discreet Virginian custom in preparing any of our ancestors for a début in electrotype, a custom which, I can assure you, has whitewashed not you alone.

Ladies and Gentlemen

Indeed, I myself could indite from memory—without consulting one single book of reference, and confining myself entirely to your paternal male line as it has fared in America since some fifty years after your demise—a volume such as Casanova, Petronius, Brantôme, and the late gifted authors of *Là-Bas* and *Only a Boy* would regard with commingled envy and blushes. But, alas, I shall never prepare any such delectable book about the Cabell family. Were there nothing else, I could not bear to leave out of it a great deal of similarly voluptuous data as to the Branch family.

Though how indeed, reflection whispers me—now that my thoughts stray from our public records to the vast cesspool of more privately preserved chronicles, well known to all genealogists—could I endure any meagre restraint to merely these two clans, when about some twenty or thirty of yet other ancient and distinguished Virginian families one could tell tales equally robust? No; here confronts me, upon all sides, an embarrassment both of prudery and of riches. Here confronts me a treasure house of luxuriant and full-flavored scandal with which no one single typewriter could ever hope to deal in one human lifetime. And here also

To Sir Richard Cabell

confronts me the probability of having to quit, with undignified haste, the State of Virginia, but a little way in advance of the lynching party improvised by the upper classes. It follows, through these considerations, that I elect to leave the private lives of our ancestors, and of all erstwhile Virginian aristocracy, in the hugger-mugger preferred by their descendants,—remarking only that the gentry have always affected their own special code of morals.

*

*　　*

—All which I confess to you, Sir, in due humbleness, since it is nowadays considered unbecoming for anyone of my countrymen to possess ancestors of any kind. Democracy permits us not even a vampire. And it is esteemed particularly un-American to possess ancestors who have for any long while resided in America—as your people have done, Sir, to their sad disadvantage—now that a so much more prolific cradle for all democratic distinction has become the steerage, with a prospering minority vote in favor of the synagogue. So, Sir Richard, the native-born gentry have fallen upon evil days; and I do not know but that, by comparison, you are well enough off in the seclusion of your pagoda.

You have, at any rate, quiet, whereas your kinsmen in Virginia are at every instant deafened and quelled, and they remain more or less intimidated, by vulgarity's shouted praise of vulgarity in conduct, and in art, and in religion, and in politics, and in all other departments of life. You are companioned, it may be, by devils: but at least the Prince of Darkness is reputed to be a gentleman, and as such, would require some atmosphere of good breeding among his attendants. The overlords of our own national polity are not quite that, and they make other demands. You are damned, it is certain: but we have no certainty of any kind, nor any special hope.

And lastly, I suppose, Sir Richard, that, although your ravening body remains alive in the tomb, yet is your soul in hell. The arrangement, doubtless, has its discomforts. Nevertheless, at this juncture one does recall Aucassin in the romance, and his frank desire to abide in hell after his death, because

To Sir Richard Cabell

"thither fare all gentlemen that are noble by nature, and all sweet courteous ladies that have two, or it may be three, lovers, besides their husbands"— whereas only the proletariat, the saint, and the deserving poor inherit heaven, said Aucassin. In brief, the young lord of Beaucaire simply could not face the thought of—after an entire lifetime spent upon earth—having to share eternity also with the ignorant, the zeal-ridden, and the blatant.

I do not say that Aucassin was right in his eschatology, of which my church does not wholly approve. I say only that, after looking about me pensively, toward all known quarters of the compass, I can well see his point.

THE SIXTEENTH LETTER:

To His Excellency
George Washington

"37th. *In Speaking to men of Quality do not lean nor look them full in the Face, nor approach too near them.*"

THE SIXTEENTH LETTER:

To His Excellency George Washington

With some slight ambiguousness, Sir, has that nation to which you stand *in loco parentis* evinced its filial piety, by making yours the most frequently met with of human faces throughout America. At first glance it might well be esteemed flattering that your portrait should adorn our dollar bills and our most often used postage stamps. Yet in its monetary form is the compliment open to question, in so far that, at the instant I write, no living creature knows what an American dollar may represent before sunset, beyond the certainty of its being something rather different to-morrow morning; nor upon consideration am I persuaded that any really reflective person would care to be commemorated on a postage stamp, which begins its career by being spat on, and ends by being punched in the face.

None the less is it fitting that your grave and wary features should grace that present puzzle, the American dollar, and that you should preside, whether in kingly scarlet or in imperial purple, over the enigmas of every day's mail. For you, when all is said, and when your innumerous biographers have striven their utmost, you remain, still, a mystery. In the aforementioned portraits your likeness to the Great Sphinx of Gizeh is plainly to be recognized; accident has a bit helped out this likeness, one grants, with the shape of your wig; and yet do you wear the resemblance justifiably. I at least, after reading I know not how many scores of books about you, books which explained you to your last least virtue and failing, find myself without any firm faith in any one of these explanations. It seems to me that with you, as with Shakespeare, it is not possible to divine your inmost nature; and that the biographers have but fumbled about both of you with countless wild gambols of guesswork.

In popular opinion, meanwhile, you endure as a sort of Americanized King Alfred—as the sublime and wise and painstakingly practical leader of a

To George Washington

great people through dark times of disaster, as one
who was always calm under fortune's malignity,
and calm too in the splendor of his ultimate
triumph. Both of you seem a bit statuesque: and, in
public imagination at least, you keep the immobil-
ity of a statue. Alfred, as the mind sees him, sits perpetually over the neatherd's scorched cakes, with
his benevolent staid face lighted by the cottage fire:
but you, Sir, kneel forever in the too celebrated
snow of Valley Forge, praying and half congealed.
We feel somehow that at no time afterward were
you ever quite thawed out.

*

*   *

Yet that also is guesswork. One does not assuredly
know anything more about you, as a human being,
than one does about Ananias or Tutankhamen. And
it follows that your relations with posterity remain
as formal and as unintimate as were your relations
with most mortals who endured the somewhat tre-
mendous moral strain of conversing with you in the
flesh.

Ladies and Gentlemen

For what, after all, can any man existent declare, with any certainty, as to the person who lived behind your Sphinx-like countenance? We know that under the grave mask lurked always a violent, nay, a verily volcanic temper, by you arduously controlled; that you were, but well knew yourself to be, undesirably slow of wit, and controlled this weakness by speaking (upon the infrequent occasions when you spoke at all) only after a majestic amount of deliberation; and that, with an incredible steadfastness, you controlled every important step in your life by the dictates of common-sense.

"Controlled" I have said three times in the one sentence: it is the word which thought associates with you inevitably. Always, and in his every function, George Washington presents the spectacle of a superb if rather stiffish gentleman exercising, in some or another form, the virtue of self-control. But against what human frailties, what soft temptings, what inner whisperings, what doubts? Well, there you leave us, once more, to guesswork. We can assert only that you lived in a perpetual, proud, and somewhat wary reserve, from which you were released just now and then by an outburst of your enormous, your deific, anger.

To George Washington

Nor, I think, could much more than this be declared, with any certainty, by any person who observed you going statelily about earth. With no man, after at any rate your boyhood had been put by, do you appear to have been even moderately familiar. It is an old story how Gouverneur Morris (with whom and Hamilton you were more nearly unbending than you were with anybody else) did once—but once only—bet that he was not afraid to slap you on the back. That deed he, with a double impiety, committed in public. You turned then, in complete silence, facing him. "The President did not speak," Morris tells us, "but the majesty of the American people was before me. Oh, his look! How I wished the floor would open and I could descend to the cellar!"

Indeed Morris records, with all seeming seriousness, that this was in his life the one occasion upon which he quailed before the glance of any mortal being. I incline to believe it not altogether a coincidence that immediately afterward Morris left the country and stayed away from America for nine years. Such, Sir, was your response to an attempt at good fellowship by one of your nearest friends; and the anecdote provokes I know not what of

233

speculation as to how glacially you must have loomed in the eyes of mere acquaintances upon frankly full-dress outings.

*

*   *

Equally, after the first fervors of boyhood, did any of womankind fail ever to dispel your reserve. Twice, it is known, you went a-wooing formally; but upon each passionate pilgrimage was your guide common-sense, and the lady an heiress born of a family a good bit outranking the Washingtons. To the other side, you do appear, in your own marmoreal fashion, to have loved irregularly, and forever a woman who was already married. You too had your lady in domnei, in so far that just once even you, the impenetrable, were touched (in your own phrase, Sir) by "the amiable beauties" of Mrs. George Fairfax of Belvoir. So, during the September of 1758, in a letter to her confirming the reports of your engagement to the wealthy widow, Mrs. Custis, you protested your complete devotion, not to Mrs. Custis but to Mrs. Fairfax, along with your undying "recollection of a thousand tender pas-

To George Washington

sages." Nobody now will ever know to just what you referred. Yet "a thousand" really does seem, in this special connection, a considerable number; and the terms you employed remain apt to exalt most handsomely the hopes of the scandal-monger.

Well, and a long forty years later, when you had but a few more months to live, we find you still writing to Mrs. Fairfax (then resident at Bath, in England) as to "those happy moments, the happiest in my life, which I have enjoyed in your company." Ah, but, Sir, but, the one trouble, the very death-stroke of romance, is that you thus confirm your undying recollection of those "thousand tender passages" in a joint letter from you and your wife, in which, after General Washington has dwelt upon his unswerving heart-hunger for Mrs. Fairfax, Mrs. Washington affably goes on to add "an account of the changes which have happened in the neighborhood" of Mount Vernon since Mrs. Fairfax resided near by at Belvoir. These two letters attest, it may be, the stability of your one serious love-affair, which seems actually to have been life-long. But you really did employ, to my finding, a somewhat angular and misplaced candor all through your sole excursion in the romantic. I can make little of a lover who declares the single-heartedness of his devotion in a letter announcing his marriage to somebody else. I can make nothing whatever of one who in restating his illicit passion employs as a collaborator his own wife. No; even *sub Venere* you continue to be an enigma; your one love-affair stays incomprehensible; and the sole safe deduction as to you and Mrs. Fairfax is that Martha Washington must have been an uncommonly sensible woman.

*

*   *

Everywhere, in brief, do you, as a person, remain a mystery and a most fit symbol of the American dollar and of the unpredictable contents of the postman's mail-bag. Yet even though your nature be hidden, we are permitted to pry some little distance into your thoughts.

For, by an odd turn, we know, and we know precisely, what you are forever thinking about on our postage stamps, and to every appearance on our dollar bills also. Gilbert Stuart himself has recorded how, when he set about painting this picture, he

236

To George Washington

"despaired of finding in that composed and quiet face any expression of the qualities which the whole world knew and might reasonably expect in a portrait." He despaired, that is, until, on an afternoon walk, the two of you met a farmer who had overreached you, Sir, in a small trading transaction. At the sight of your quondam swindler "the spirit of the General and the President leaped forth"—and, to Mr. Stuart's vast joy, your features took on just the expression which he needed and has faithfully preserved for posterity upon our two- and three-cent stamps.

In brief, Sir, you endure among us in the attitude of a gentleman who is conscious of having been swindled. And I, for one, I would very much prefer to regard the fact as an unexplained dispensation of Providence, that at every turn our Democracy should be faced by the Father of the Country in this particular frame of mind.

Far more than any other man you contributed to our making as a nation: without any dissent the Republic acclaims you its founder. Yet is it true that the régime which you meant to perpetuate was but an extension of the benevolent Virginian oligarchy into which you, Sir, had so stiffly and reso-

237

lutely climbed, to become its chief ornament. And your opinion as to any lackwit who put faith in the French poisons of Democracy you were at pains, during the latter part of your life, to express with exactitude: "My opinion is that you could as soon scrub the blackamoor white as to change the principle of a professed Democrat, and that he will leave nothing unattempted to overthrow the government of this country."

So I am afraid there is no getting around the fact that you expected to have the national and local affairs of America administered by the gentry of America. Not to foresee the future is very often the reward of self-sacrifice, one rejoices to note. And it occurs to me that if ever, in the fashion of Macbeth, you had been granted a vision of your successors in the Presidency, you would for no long while have retained the relatively mild purple tints which you wear on our postage stamps. . . . But at this point I shudder; and hastily I dismiss the too harrowing mental picture. One cannot bear to think of George Washington as being thus bedevilled by a Polk or a Johnson, or thus haunted by a Hayes and a Harding. One feels—somehow—that in any such circumstances the Sphinx would

To George Washington

once more have spoken, deifically and without
restraint.

No (I conclude), the remarks of George Washington when confronted by his successors are remarks which simply do not bear thinking about. So
I elect instead, Sir, to think about your achievements. They were stupendous: for you created
that vast America which the rest of the world to-
day contemplates, if not exactly with unbridled
envy, at least with appropriate emotions. Your work
endures, forever increasingly. And yet no hour
passes wherein I do not find you observing your
life's work, your so laboriously fashioned and your
so incredible creation, with the countenance of a
very great, grave gentleman who has been swindled.
It is a fact from which I prefer to educe no moral.

THE SEVENTEENTH LETTER:

To Edgar Allan Poe, Esq.

"To take him with more than a certain degree of seriousness is to lack seriousness oneself. An enthusiasm for Poe is the mark of a decidedly primitive stage of reflection."

THE SEVENTEENTH LETTER:

To Edgar Allan Poe, Esq.

Some ninety years ago, Sir, in commenting upon
The Quacks of Helicon, you remarked on the circumstance that, "as a literary people, we are one
vast perambulating humbug." Yet even to-day
there are beings who protest that your genius was
of an exotic nature which did not interpret the
American spirit directly. For my part, I think that
this one statement established you as the first of all
realists in the field of American letters. And I rather
fear that upon this occasion you voiced an eternal
verity.

I must tell you, Sir, that still the considerate person, whensoever he regards that legion of soul-
chilling volumes which, for lack of a better term

and in view of our prudish postal laws, we by ordinary describe in print as "American literature," becomes flatly bewildered. It does not appear humanly possible that a country of such size and variety, and blessed with a history so eventful, should have produced during three hundred years, with the sole exception of Edgar Allan Poe, not one true literary genius.

Meanwhile the great bulk of American literature exists, as a visible and frightening spectacle, in our public libraries. In the quiet stack room one may walk about (arm in arm, as it were, with awe) among many-colored, solid, and quite impenetrable walls of Coopers and Hawthornes and Melvilles, of Longfellows and Whittiers and Whitmans, and of yet other American literary classics. Nobody ever disturbs them, I am told, except an occasional wretched schoolchild, for whom they are "required reading." At all other seasons they rest unmoved in this hushed mausoleum of mediocrity . . . I regarded them morbidly. I have actually read these books, I reflected, in a remote time as dead now as the time in which these books were written. I remembered their contents. Then I shivered slightly. I tiptoed away. It was a relief to get back into the sun-lighted distributing room, where the general public thronged about the Mysteries shelf and in smaller numbers were inspecting the Latest New Novels section.

*

*　*

None the less it seems probable that these books are still read here and there, if only by the professorial who write yet other books about them. Recalling this grim possibility, one is tempted to demand of the welkin how much of this sad stuff can an adult mind regard seriously? And to any such desperate demands the welkin (if in one of its relatively infrequent conversational moods) would reply, I am certain:

"A sufficing amount of Poe; and a tiny fraction of Mark Twain. All other 'classic' American writers—as one should say, from Washington Irving down to Henry James—when they are considered separately, compel a common verdict. You can declare only, 'The man lacked genius.' A majority of these writers have been at needless pains to emphasize their defects by writing atrociously. None has mastered a really good prose style. But at all times the trouble with any one of these elder American writers is plain enough when you appraise him without prejudice and—as the learned remark—*sub specie æternitatis.* Here is this or that talent, more or less creditably exercised, but here simply is not genius, that gift through default of which (in a world already blessed with more literary masterpieces than can be read comfortably during one lifetime) any writer becomes negligible in short order."

In brief, Sir, the welkin, which at odd times has looked down upon all American writers, retains that attitude; and in consequence the welkin would have to agree with you that, as a literary people, we from the first have been "one vast perambulating humbug." We have done (as, at varying periods, did Carthage, and Egypt, and I daresay Venezuela and Andorra likewise) our patriotic utmost to bring forth a creditable literature. Year after year we have loyally cried up, at the top of our national lungs, this or the other American writer as a supreme genius. And then, slowly, sickeningly, but inevitably, has dawned the perception that he was nothing of the sort. He had done his very best, poor man; and so had we. But he simply happened not to have been born with genius, and by-and-by there was no longer any hiding the omission.

*

*   *

Now you, Sir, did happen, beyond sane dispute, to be born a genius. Exceedingly small comfort you got out of this happening; nor did your genius, I make bold to think, produce much which was wholly worthy of your genius. The point is that, in you, America was demonstrably granted one literary genius. The point is, moreover, that what has happened once may, at any rate, conceivably, happen again.

Indeed, for aught I know to the contrary, it may already have happened. I trust that no living author may view these remarks as disparaging to his—or, above all, to her—most praiseworthy productions. It may well be that among the American writers who have flourished during the twentieth century yet another authentic literary genius or so has been

247

produced. As to this possibility I dare venture no opinion. I have written a great deal about those of my contemporaries whom for various reasons I had enjoyed reading. But here enters the personal element: most of them were my friends, and a good part of the interest aroused in me by this or the other book arose from the unliterary reason that it was written by So-and-so. In brief, I have always recognized that no writer can appraise with fairness, or even with common-sense, his contemporaries. He is unavoidably biassed by his liking, or it may be by his dislike, of the person who wrote the book he is criticizing.

Nobody should know this better than you do, Sir, whose repose in your present Elysium—but I entreat your pardon, for I had meant of course to say your Aidenn—cannot possibly be unworried, just now and then, by this or the other embarrassing recollection of your critical dicta during your sad and troubled stay on this planet. I do not mean those stinging unfavorable criticisms which kept you in perpetual hot water. Posterity has well justified these. But one does rather hope that you recall remorsefully the encomia which you once lavished upon the mild merits of Mesdames Hemans, Baillie,

To Edgar Allan Poe

Landon, Norton, Whitman, and Osgood; and that even in eternal bliss you find time to blush a bit over your gallant hailings of far too "many a poetaster in petticoats" as pre-eminent servitors of Apollo.

*

* *

Howsoever this may be, Sir, I confess that, of late years, I have read very few new American books, and so may not pretend to inform you whether the present abundance of literary genius among us is at all times correctly reported by its admiring publishers. An author, it is my experience, comes to read less and less. I, at least, at an age denied to you by tribulation and alcohol, I appear to have reached, without being proffered any alternative save the dark and tranquillizing ministrations of the funeral parlor, that stage in life when reading is not any more an assured diversion. My eyes tire very easily nowadays, even when perusing the most shocking sentiments; my memory so plagues me that I remember the *genre* and the climax of virtually all our new fiction before ending the third chapter; and I perceive that I have read as many books as I care to read, in any honest sense of that verb, by which I mean the deliberate assimilation of a book from its title page to its colophon.

*

*   *

It follows that, whensoever people talk about "literature," I look back with incredulous wonder on my former exploits, on my forced marches and prolonged sieges, in the way of reading. Upon such occasions I recall (with a proper pride) such prodigies, let us say, as my unfaltering slow conquest of each canto of *The Faerie Queene*; of some eight volumes of the Shelburne Essays even as they were written by Dr. Paul E. More; of Chaucer's every, most illiterately spelled line (in addition to the Preliminary Essay, the Memoir, the Introduction, and all the footnotes, even as they were written by the Reverend W. W. Skeat, M. A.) ; of Milton's Collected Works; of one whole novel by Ludwig Lewisohn; and of Adelaide Anne Procter's *Legends*

To Edgar Allan Poe

and Lyrics—without my having pusillanimously skipped one word in any of these dreadful productions.

Nor does that harrowing list record one-tenth of one per cent. of my self-inflicted discomforts. When people talk about "literature" I recall likewise that, as go the world's drearier "literary classics," I seem to have read some part of all books, or in any event of all books existent in English, that have any claims to be called important, howsoever many hundreds of them I never happened to finish. Even our depressing American "classics," as I but now hinted, I once managed to read dauntlessly all the way through. I sigh over this reflection, making the customary reference to good Cynara: and I return (more or less) to the subject in hand.

For I estimate roughly, my dear Mr. Poe, that, as a result of all this time-wasting, I to-day remain upon visiting terms, as it were, with at utmost a thousand volumes, to which I elect now and again to return, as one seeks out a familiar friend, informally and briefly, reading only a page or two, and then putting aside the book with the frankness permissible between old associates. That contents me, as goes the obsolescent practice of reading. And

Ladies and Gentlemen

I have no true desire to hobnob with any other authors—either living or dead, whether immortal or
merely American.

*

* *

With your books, Sir, I became familiar in early
childhood. You may perhaps recall—in your Aidenn
—the young Robert Cabell who was your schoolfellow in Richmond, at the English and Classical
School conducted by Joseph H. Clarke, and later
by William Burk. In your once celebrated swimming exploit in the James river, when during the
June of 1824 you swam from Ludlam Wharf to
Warwick Bar, a distance of six miles, Robert Cabell
accompanied you throughout this adventure, with
the appreciable difference that, while you were
swimming, he kept abreast of you in a row boat.
That prudent lad was my grandfather. So uncon-
ventional was he in the rôle of an author's schoolfellow, however, that in later life he read every one
of your books, and even praised them. To your
Black Cat, Sir, he introduced me when I was eight
or thereabouts, by the logical process of remarking

To Edgar Allan Poe

that he did not think a little boy ought to read it until somewhat older; and my grandfather Cabell thus led me to sup deep on horrors, because I read forthwith your complete writings, in the above-mentioned thorough-going fashion, and disposed of five quarto volumes hand-running.

I cannot promise you ever to repeat the achievement. I cannot even assert that nowadays I find your horrors to be quite as blood-freezing as are your allegedly humorous stories. Still, to your books, almost alone of our American "classics," I note that I do yet return from time to time. And as it happens, I read with a peculiar interest, only last week, your justly famous short story *Berenice*, which begins, in so near as I may quote from memory:

"Misery is manifold. The fair land of promise lately looming on the horizon is again enveloped in impenetrable mists, and again the wretchedness of earth is multiform. Overreaching the wide horizon as the rainbow, the hues of misery are as various as the hues of that arch—as distinct too, yet as intimately blended—and beneath its spectral brilliancies the undersigned is Crushed. Overreaching the wide horizon as a rainbow! Ay, but hope has sunk beneath the horizon, and forever withdrawn from the eyes of a drifting wretch whose Doom is sealed. How is it that from beauty I have derived a type of unloveliness—from the covenant of peace a smile of sorrow? In short, my dear Copperfield, hiding the ravages of care with a sickly mask of mirth, I did not inform you this evening that the bolt is impending and the tree must fall."

At this point, Sir, it occurred to me that I must be confusing your *Berenice* with the writings of some other author. I wondered what other strangely gifted being could have written in a prose style so closely resembling the style of Edgar Allan Poe that in recollection I should be jumbling extracts from both of you? Then, as I strove to recall your second paragraph, all became plain. For the story continued—or so it seemed to me—to this general effect:

"My baptismal name is Wilkins: that of my family I will not mention. Yet there are no towers in one of the provincial towns of our favored island more time-honored than are my gloomy, gray hereditary halls, and my ashes, at no distant period, will probably be found in the cemetery attached to this venerable pile, for which the spot to which I refer

To Edgar Allan Poe

has acquired a reputation, shall I say from China to Peru?"

And with that, the riddle was solved. With that, I perceived my grandfather Cabell had among your schoolmates a predecessor truly illustrious. The circumstance had become evident that when, a bit earlier, Mr. John Allan entered you at the Manor House School, at Stoke Newington, in England, you attended (shall I say) the same institution of learning as Master Wilkins Micawber; and that the two of you (still, shall I say) quaffed from the same font of Helicon, in the time that each was forming his notions of sublime writing under the same tutor. The result in Master Micawber's case was highly successful: but it would have been far better for the forlorn cause of American literature, I reflected, had Master Poe been instructed by some other pedagogue.

Luckily for everybody concerned, you do not always write in the exact vein of your English schoolmate. My point here is merely that it is astounding to find in the practitioner of any such "Gothic" inflations (in which your prose abounds) the pronouncer of that just verdict, "As a literary people, we are one vast perambulating humbug."

Ladies and Gentlemen

For what, just what, my dear Mr. Poe, could have
been your precise conception of humbug in the precise instant that you were writing such trite and un-
abashed and long-winded balderdash about the fair
land of promise, and the rainbow of misery, and the
covenant of peace, and so on? Wherein, Sir (simply
between ourselves) does your "smile of sorrow"
differ from your former schoolfellow's "sickly mask
of mirth," except that he somewhat excels you here
at your own game of magniloquence? And does not
his venerable pile, which has acquired a reputation
from China to Peru, stand rather uncomfortably
near to your gloomy, gray, and hereditary halls,
than which no towers are more time-honored, *et
cætera,* and so forth? For my part, I cannot but think
of each building as a stucco parsonage attached to
the Temple of Humbug—that deity in whose service both you and Micawber officiate as high priests
upon a distressing number of occasions.

*

* *

To the other side, Sir, I praise you because you
gave to what sophomores and the radical weeklies

256

still describe as "the American scene" exactly the attention it deserved from an artist. You lived—it is the astounding fact—in the America visited by young Martin Chuzzlewit and Mark Tapley. In letters your confrères were Messrs. La Fayette Kettle and Putnam Smif and Mrs. Hominy and Mr. Jefferson Brick. You observed your fair quota of "the most remarkable men in our country," let none doubt, with appreciation. But, for the simple reason that you were born a genius, you knew that a truthful representation of his own era and of his own native surroundings is the one indulgence which has been avoided by the true literary artist since Homer's prime. You relinquished your contemporaries, in brief, to the casual mercies of Mr. Charles Dickens, who, being blessed with both foreign birth and a sense of humor, was able to accord them Jeddart justice along with an assured immortality.

I praise you, in fine, because, as it has been observed of Edgar Allan Poe, by one of his more intelligent critics: "There are few examples in the whole range of his writings of a single normal interest in the world in which he lived . . . There is not, in the ordinary sense, one iota of observation or touch of reality in any story or poem which he produced. No native characters, no observed incidents, no contemporary problems appear; into himself he drew nothing, but he poured out, on the contrary, scenes, characters, and emotions which had no source but his own imagination, no relation to any except the visionary world of which he was the only inhabitant."

You preferred—as one may say without immodesty—your own private Poictesme, an impressive, a preternatural, and a laughterless kingdom. You esteemed that in this way the truly great creative genius should create his own arena, well to the farther side of reality. And you proved it.

*

* *

In brief, America has produced just one literary genius whose existence the world recognizes; and once only during the exercise of his genius did he fully recognize the existence of America. That—I regret to say—was when he remarked, "As a literary people, we are one vast perambulating humbug."

To Edgar Allan Poe

—Which recalls me, Sir, to my real theme. I would but remind you it was a good ninety years ago that you reached this conclusion. I would but assure you that to-day the ever-widening, the enormous field of American letters in very little resembles that starveling literary province wherein you (upon the whole) did not flourish. That the Republic nowadays pullulates with literary ability of the very first order is a circumstance daily attested by our columnists, by our literary supplements, by our Pulitzer prize winners, by the rosters of both the National Academy and the National Institute of Arts and Letters, by our publishers' advertisements, and by yet other authorities to whom you, I am certain, if you were yet alive, would (in a stage of senility so far advanced) yield every suitable sort of deference.

Literature, in brief, has become with us of America a huge organized hubbub, in which everybody involved is doing his fond utmost to play at appraising with entire seriousness the fourth rate. No matter, Sir, how imposingly resounds this hubbub, none in the, as it were, racket takes the game gravely, from his own private standpoint: at utmost, he may bear in mind the off-chance that some of the

Ladies and Gentlemen

other participants may be really in earnest. And so, publishing season after publishing season, we go on loyally crying up, at the top of our national lungs, this or the other American writer as a supreme genius; and then tacitly, with the onset of the next publishing season, we let drop all thought of his genius, or even of the man's continued existence, in the while that we acclaim somebody else just as strenuously and with the same private scepticism.

I regard, for example, the tributes which are being paid at this instant to one of our current "best sellers." If I do not name it, that is but because the negligible is best left anonymous. The book is a mild imitation of *Gil Blas*: and no literate being would pretend, in the sanity of calm conversation, that the book is important one way or the other. But in print, Sir, we chaunt a quite different anthem. The *Atlantic Monthly*, I perceive, is unable to think of any other novel that ranges so far and yet is so solidly observed or imagined in every part, or one that more perfectly combines the freedom and charm of romance with the sense of fact of realism. The New York *Times* declares it essentially a story, and a very great story, by a creative humanist. The *Herald Tribune* ranks it as a really extraor-

260

To Edgar Allan Poe

dinary book. The New York *Evening Post* finds it
a romantic and magnificent landmark in American
fiction which marks its author as the most potent of
American novelists living or dead.

—All which Yankee understatement and stiff self-
restraint is in contrast to the more gratifyingly out-
spoken verdict of the Los Angeles *Times*, that this
is the most perfectly conceived and exquisitely designed novel ever written, a volume which will
grip the reader with its fascinations,—and, in short,
a narrative which the Los Angeles *Times* guaran-
tees to be an immortal book that vibrates and sings
itself into the very marrow of the bones.

Though the meaning here may seem a trifle obscure, or even osteocopic, about the reviewer's good
intentions there can be little doubt. And we acclaim,
I assure you, my dear Mr. Poe, dozens upon dozens
of books every month in very much the same astounding high terms, through our loyal desire to
encourage that literary genius who, as yet, has not
come forward to fill your place. We still seek to
bring forth a creditable American literature
through a conjunction of the tomtom and the trum-
pet, in default of that recalcitrant great writer who,
for some reason or another reason, declines to be

born among us as your rightful successor. And it does not appear suitable, Sir, that into any din so conscientious you—as the one American literary genius whom the world acknowledges—should at any time obtrude your croaking, in the harsh fashion of your own unoptimistic Raven, "As a literary people, we are one vast perambulating humbug."

THE EIGHTEENTH LETTER:

To Mr. John Wilkes Booth

"The fame of Mr. Wilkes Booth has preceded him, and we cheerfully add our mite of admiration to the general praise which has greeted his efforts."

THE EIGHTEENTH LETTER:

To Mr. John Wilkes Booth

It is necessary to remember that you were very much of the theatre. You were born of a family of which every member was an actor: you yourself at twenty-two were a star; and you became forthwith that strange creature which we have since learned to describe as a matinée idol, some while before matinées had come into being. All your brief life was spent in and about theatres: and your life reached its climax there when, during the third act of a comedy, you killed Abraham Lincoln in a crowded theatre, leaped down from out of the President's box to your accustomed place behind the footlights, shouted, *"Sic semper tyrannis!"* and thus made your last bow to the public.

Ladies and Gentlemen

The whole affair is incredible. Nay, it is operatic. One almost wonders that you did not follow up the assassination with an aria, inasmuch as the performance was so openly purloined from Signor Verdi's then recent opera, *Un Ballo in Maschera.* None of it, in fine, could possibly have happened, one feels, except in opera or perhaps in the more extravagant kinds of melodrama.

Thereafter you vanish into large clouds of surmise, pursued (to be accurate) by ten thousand cavalrymen and twenty-five hundred policemen. I record these figures because I am sure it would have pleased you, at your heart's bottom, to know how many persons went a-hunting after John Wilkes Booth. You were trapped, says history, in the Garrett barn, near Port Royal in Virginia: and whether you committed suicide there, or were shot down by Boston Corbett, remains open to debate, because both facts were fully proven by witnesses under oath. The self-made eunuch who asserted that he had ended your living, I may here mention, was later declared insane, upon the rather unsufficing grounds that he attempted to kill off the State Legislature of Kansas.

At all events, you were duly buried at the arsenal

266

To John Wilkes Booth

in Washington, after this dual death: and that yet
later you should have arisen from your grave, upon
several occasions, in the forms of John St. Helen
and of David E. George and of Rev. Dr. J. G. Arm-
strong, and of still other persons, seems appropriate
enough, in view of the improbability which dis-
tinguishes all your doings.

*

*   *

Now I, Sir, was reared to think of you with extreme charity. You had been popular in Richmond
when you postured there, throughout two theatrical
seasons, as the leading man in Mr. Kunkel's stock
company, just before the War Between the States.
My maternal grandparents had known you, and remembered you, not as an assassin but as an admired
dramatic genius. I can well recall the small and
sweepingly signed *carte de visite* photograph of you
(seated, with more than ambrosial curls, a horn-
handled cane, and a wholly implausible amount of
watch chain festooned about your plaid waistcoat),
that portrait which my grandmother Branch treas-

ured. She spoke of you at all times, I must report, as a young man who at utmost had acted injudiciously, for her opinion of Mr. Lincoln remained unreconstructed.

Moreover, I yet possess the pack of cards which you sent to my grandfather, Lieutenant Colonel James R. Branch of the Army of Northern Virginia, after the outbreak of hostilities. That they were manufactured by Goodall & Son, London, I gather from the ace of spades, which is a tranquillized adaptation of the arms of Great Britain, wherein at each side the lion and the unicorn, after two and a half centuries of rampancy, have lain down for a well-merited rest. The backs of these cards are adorned with the national flag, the battle flag, and the seal, of the Confederacy, presented in red and blue and a white now turned into ivory yellow. Handling these cards, which you once handled, I wonder how your generation managed to play whist, let us say, without any small figure in the corner of each card: but otherwise I do find these cards to be a proof of your erstwhile existence. By their tangibility I am persuaded that you did, in mere point of fact, once live and tread visibly the streets of the same Richmond to which I nowadays

To John Wilkes Booth

yield taxes and jury service, even though my fancy lacks the requisite wild vigor quite to believe in you.

*

*   *

I know too that (again, in mere point of fact) you came near changing the course of American history. Perhaps you did change it. I think not. But in any case you came near changing it in a quite different way. With such industry has your story been hushed up that not many persons remember the zeal, the patience, and the skill, with which you attempted to abduct that Abraham Lincoln whom in the outcome you—from the standpoint of art, at least—far more felicitously murdered.

But at abduction your luck was villainous. When Edwin Forrest was performing at Ford's Theatre, in the January of 1864, all was arranged for you and your seven accomplices to seize the President of the United States when, after the play, he departed homeward attended by but a single guard. The sole, the unforeseeable hitch in the working out of your plot was that a sudden severe rainstorm prevented the President from leaving the White House that evening. You tried once more, when the President was scheduled to visit a theatrical entertainment for the wounded soldiers at the Seventh Street Hospital. Through predestination, it might seem, Mrs. Lincoln had one of her uncontrollable tantrums that afternoon, and the President dared not leave her. In this way did the very winds of heaven and the variability of women unite against you steadfastly, Sir, as an abductor.

Then yet again were your plans laid and perfected, in the March of 1865, when the President was to drive out to the Soldiers' Home near Washington to witness a performance by Lester Wallack. Sheer accident foiled you once more. Lincoln was detained, at the very last moment, by the coming of delayed dispatches from General Grant; and Lincoln hastily sent his Chief Justice to represent him at the evening's presentation of *Still Waters Run Deep*. Your company surrounded the carriage precisely as you had planned: but you found it occupied only by Salmon P. Chase, who was not the least bit to your purpose.

Well, Sir—but for that rainstorm, but for that tantrum, but for the so theatrically pat arrival of

To John Wilkes Booth

those dispatches—it is tempting to imagine what might have happened. Had the eight of you seized Lincoln during any one of these three attempts to capture him, there need have been no great difficulty in getting your drugged prisoner across the Potomac, and so to Richmond, the as yet unfallen capital of the Confederacy. You and your accomplice Herold crossed the Potomac easily enough after you had killed Lincoln. As to what would have followed the success of your planned *coup d'état* I dare venture no guess. With the President of the United States in the hands of the Confederate government in January 1864, the war almost certainly would have forestalled a recent cliché by ending in a peace without victory. With Lincoln captured in the March of 1865, the fighting would probably have gone on until the already exhausted Confederacy had succumbed. But in either event art would have been impoverished.

*

*   *

For the point is that, had you prospered in abduction, there would have been no Lincoln myth.

271

Ladies and Gentlemen

The point is that, had you succeeded in your pro-
posed adaptation from Dumas *père,* by abducting
Lincoln just as d'Artagnan abducted General
Monk, then the North, as a whole, would have regarded Lincoln as a minor politician of whom the
North was tolerably well rid. The man was not yet
popular, he was not yet respected. He was indeed at
no time regarded with much seriousness until you,
Sir, on a sudden made him important by killing
him. Through your sole derringer did Abraham
Lincoln become a sublime myth, at precisely
twenty-two minutes after seven o'clock in the morning of 15 April 1865, when Secretary Stanton (who
had aforetime declared himself to be perpetually
inconvenienced by "the painful imbecility of
Lincoln") arose from the dead President's bedside,
in the Petersons' theatrical boarding house, to remark in suitably histrionic terms, "Now he belongs
to the ages."

I pause here to observe that your victim, after
having thrice eluded you on the way to a theatrical
performance, and after having been shot by you in
a theatre, died later in a theatrical boarding house,
lying across the same bed which you had formerly
occupied in this house. There is no severing you

To John Wilkes Booth

from the theatre. And out of all the beds in Washington, Abraham Lincoln died in the bed of John Wilkes Booth. Here again we face an event which, one feels, could not possibly have happened except in the more extravagant kinds of melodrama.

*

*   *

—All which has, nowadays, nothing to do with your plain right to be acclaimed supreme among American creative artists. As I have suggested in another place, fate sees to it that for every nation is created, in its youth, its own special autochthonous mythology. It appears to me that Captain John Smith was the first of our great mythopœic geniuses, and Parson Weems the second: of Pocahontas and of George Washington they made excellent heroic figures. A bit later the various founding Fathers of the Republic were edited and augmented by still other romanticists. Yet each one of these artists began with a promising and rich stock of raw material. Yours, Sir, is the unique distinction of having created a great national symbol out of the whole cloth. All the facts were against you: even now it stays an awkward circumstance that every contemporary record as to the flesh-and-blood Lincoln should be more or less at odds with that Abraham Lincoln whom your pistol shot created and whom our nation quite justly reveres.

Nevertheless may we who admire your romance-making refuse to think about the actual backwoods politician whom you killed, or to grant the not very edifying trickeries which you ended. Unreason is at all times one of the happier privileges of patriotism. I at least, as a whole-hearted romanticist, I am completely in favor of ignoring the mere facts about Abraham Lincoln. I prefer cordially to acclaim the great Lincoln myth, as an invaluable American possession. Already it has begotten some fine statuary and painting; it provides us one and all with a holiday on the twelfth of each February; and it has enriched every department of literature. It remains to-day a continual inspiration to the young, teaching that the most humble may rise to eminence, that supreme virtues may lurk under the most repulsive exteriors, and, in fine, that the usual copy-book mottoes may be regarded with seriousness. Such beliefs make both for private hope and

To John Wilkes Booth

for national tranquillity. Then too it is plain that the effect of this myth upon posterity cannot well fail to be even more beneficial and more lively, when once the last inconvenient fact about Abraham Lincoln has been comfortably forgotten, and your sublime creation has been enthroned for good and all in the adroitly adjusted lights of approved history.

Meanwhile I lament the injustice done to you, Sir, in that your masterwork should still appear unsigned at best, or, at worst, be attributed to Jehovah. It is as yet a bit too soon, I suppose, to dismiss the moral aspects of murder. Pending this assured outcome, the considerate person may find comfort in reflecting that from the artist, from the truly great artist, in any branch of æsthetics, time has always removed any stigma of this modish and transitory sort.

Nobody is really bothered nowadays by the two murders in which Villon was involved, or by Leonardo's homosexuality, or by Wagner's excursions into adultery. Instead, we take gratefully the fine art which was colored by, or perhaps resulted from, these same sins. And in the long run, I would

275

like to believe, mankind may come somewhat similarly to recognize its indebtedness to John Wilkes
Booth.

*

*   *

It is not profitless, Sir, in this place to summarize
our accredited knowledge of Lincoln as, the more
thanks to your artistry, it survives in man's general
belief. Abraham Lincoln was born in humble circumstances, in a mere barn, thitherto used as a
stable. His nominal father was a carpenter: it is con-
tended that, in point of fact, his real father was a
person of considerably higher station. Abraham
Lincoln was a reformer, maligned and abused by
his perverse people. He was a seer and a prophet,
foreknowing his own cruel doom, yet remaining
always calm and meek and patient. He was sad-
dened by the knowledge that he, who labored
through self-immolation to redeem mankind from
its sins, had come to bring not peace but a sword.
He was killed, treacherously, upon Good Friday:

and was duly buried. A little while afterward his sepulchre was found to be vacant.

Here and there this legend, it may be, seems not wholly original. As a late comer among the nations, America has had to adapt a great deal of its mythology from far older sources. None the less does this splendid myth, which you Americanized with a pistol, well satisfy a great people's need; and it inculcates steadily among us every one of the standard virtues, so that your self-sacrifice has fostered both art and morals.

Well, and what follows? Merely, Sir, that the gratitude of a republic yet merits its place in proverb. But for you, this Abraham Lincoln, after enduring the experiences of Andrew Johnson, would have occupied very much the position which Johnson now occupies in popular esteem, as possessing not even the low-grade abilities displayed by an average President of the United States. You gave us, in place of the dingy truth, a demi-god and a national messiah. But instead of that gratitude which you had earned, we have repaid with obloquy the most great of America's creative artists.

THE NINETEENTH LETTER:

To Jeanne Antoinette Poisson Le
Normant d'Étioles, Marquise
de Pompadour

"But where is the Pompadour too?
This was the pompadour's fan."

THE NINETEENTH LETTER:

*To Jeanne Antoinette Poisson Le Normant
d'Étioles, Marquise de Pompadour*

You were called more simply, Madame, in the days of your power, "the Pompadour": and it appears odd that I also should remember the reign of the pompadour, not over clearly, but very fondly, and even with some hint of nostalgia. For in those days, it seems to me, the pompadour was the badge —or, as one might more justly say, the bright and most splendid crown—of a semi-divine race who did not strikingly resemble the young women in current use nowadays.

It was an idyllic period, which might be termed pastoral but for the infrequency of its black sheep. Victoria still reigned in England, and the polite life of America likewise was governed by Victorianism.

Ladies and Gentlemen

All skeletons stayed sedately in their own proper closets; sepulchres were quite liberally whitened; and the extreme limit of printed impropriety was, I imagine, the not scarlet, the merely pink, iniquities of that always dog-eared *Police Gazette* which one met with in barber shops—whither none of the fair sex (as they were still called, here and there) ever penetrated . . . Nor indeed was it then mentally possible to think about any really nice woman in connection with the unrestraint and déshabille of a barber shop. Gentlewomen, in those times, were respected as beings who yet kept about them something of the fading and final radiance of domnei, its thin, faint, but beguiling afterglow. In brief, except only in barber shops, in saloons, and in clubs, there were ladies all over the place—which is almost like saying that in my own day I have noted the Great Auk or the pterodactyl as a familiar feature of the American landscape.

And it appears droll that, at a time when the professed standards of that now extinct creature, the lady, were at their supreme highest, the crowning ornament of the lady should have been the pompadour. For you, Madame, were not—upon the whole—in complete accord with Victorianism; and

To Madame de Pompadour

to imitate you was, at the very least, to acknowledge
the existence of that sort of person whose existence
ladies simply did not acknowledge . . . I do not
know how they circumvented this point in logic.
I know only that in practice they did imitate you,
through the aid of much mystic paraphernalia,
which included wholly unrodent-like "rats."

*

*   *

They imitated, in fine, that rolled-back and that
puffed-out arrangement of your thinning hair, as
you are yet to be seen, Madame, in the portrait
called *La Belle Jardinière*, which Carlo Van Loo
painted of the King's *maîtresse en titre* when Louis
Quinze ruled nominally in France, and you ruled
in reality . . . And this style of hair dressing the
ladies termed, in your honor, "the pompadour."
Such, then, is your ultimate glory, Madame: your
fair ghost appeared, like a benevolent fairy, at the
cradle side of the newborn twentieth century, to
bestow upon it the pompadour; and the last living
lady (whosoever she may have been) was your faithful mimic, in at any event her coiffure.

Ladies and Gentlemen

To survive as a style of hair dressing may seem a strange fate: and yet it is less than singular. There was your predecessor in royal dalliance, for example, La Vallière: she endures as a trinket. Just so does the urbane Chesterfield live on, more variously, as a sofa, and a chest of drawers, and a cigarette. Of those two great generals who met at Waterloo, Wellington became boots, and Napoleon a pastry. Scarcely could the British commander-in-chief during the Crimean War have expected that, with so much of military glory to his credit, only the cut of his overcoat would to-day be remembered, as the Raglan.

Nor, I imagine, did John Montagu, when he had brought to him, at the card table, meat between two slices of bread, so that he could eat without interrupting the game, know that in this easy fashion he was winning eternal fame. The fourth Earl of Sandwich may well have thought that to have been postmaster general, and secretary of state, and first lord of the admiralty, and so on—to have played godfather to a whole group of Pacific islands—and in addition to all this, to have afforded England "an administration unique for corruption and incapacity"—that these (he may quite conceivably have

To Madame de Pompadour

thought) were achievements of graver importance than was any mere makeshift for uninterrupted gambling. Yet, if so, how gravely was John Montagu mistaken! for how generously, upon how many menus, and with what strange and surprising interiors, is the great name of Sandwich honored to-day in our road houses and our drugstores . . . But I divagate.

*

* *

And you rebuke me, Madame. Pallid, and frail, and extremely lovely, you arise before me (as in your portrait by Latour) clothed in white satin embroidered with rosebuds, with large lace sleeves, with a beribboned corsage of ineffably vague violet tints. Your slippers are pink; in your rolled-back and puffed-out, chestnut-colored hair there is just a dash of powder; beneath it, your fair and delicate face appears coolly scornful. You do not relish this nonsense which remembers you merely as a coiffure. It does not merit perhaps a *lettre de cachet*, not immediately. None the less do you wish to remind me—without any least irritation, in view of my complete insignificance—that beneath this coiffure, as to which I prattle, moved a superb and unscrupulous brain.

I grant that very willingly, Madame. You were cold; you were grasping to an extent which was thought remarkable even in the daughter of an absconded tax-collector; your cunning was serpent-like: you had no least technical virtue, except only, it may be, your love of art and of art's more delicate products. You did love beauty, or, at any rate, prettiness. Its presence awakened in you always—in you, the frigid, the unwilling, the unutterably tired harlot—something of warmth and of active kindliness, as did nothing else in this world perhaps, and as, very certainly, did no human creature in this world at any time. You appear to have loved no flesh-and-blood being, not even temperately . . . You were a bit irritated, it is true, by the death of your only child, because you had but lately arranged to marry Alexandrine to the Duc de Chaulnes, who would have brought into your family circle his three million francs. Your daughter's death thus became to you a real loss, which you felt arithmetically . . . For the rest, you despised, naturally enough, the

To Madame de Pompadour

nobility and the gentry who thronged about you, the enthroned tax-collector's daughter, as your suppliants. You at bottom despised also your Louis Quinze, just as he at bottom came by-and-by to dislike fretfully, and to fear most profoundly, you.

Even from the first, one imagines, you had coolly despised Louis the Well-Loved. But you had need of him. So, when but a girl of twenty-two, you, who were born a nobody, and thus lacked the entrée at court, you pursued this petulant but all-powerful King whensoever he quitted the protection of his palace to hunt in the woods of Sénart. Every day you indomitably hunted the hunter, incomparable in your rose-pink gowns, and most elegantly mounted in your fine phaeton lined with blue silk, until—after rather more than a year of ungallant evasion—he capitulated.

Thus did you take his kingdom. You conquered your Louis Quinze, through the sheer weight of your persistence; and for nineteen years you held the unwilling, the restive lecher, even down to the day of your death, with your not-ever-failing adroitness . . . He was delighted to be rid of you, remarking affably, as your funeral cortège drove off in the rain, "Madame has a bad day for her journey." But he had not ever the pluck to resist you, living . . . So, for nineteen years, did the Pompadour govern France absolutely, and rob the exchequer every day with both hands: it is a record, I grant, unequalled by any other woman . . . Yes, very truly, Madame, you were a deal more than a coiffure, you were unspeakably more than a season's mode in hair dressing: for you, who died childless, became by-and-by the mother of I know not how many revolutions.

You were a most dreadful, a most petty, and yet, in your own special patched and berouged way, a remarkably great personage. Like Mélusine, in a romance which seems once to have been more familiar to me than it is nowadays, you were a terrible and delicious woman.

Ah, but, Madame—as the three mullahs said of Lord Timur, and as the knights who had flagged in their quest of the Sangreal said of yet somebody else—that was a long while ago. It does not really matter any more. And in this world we, being what we are, can feel deeply about only this or the other transitory occurrence which we have perceived with our own senses. For this reason am I perforce led now and then to think, a bit fondly, about the reign

To Madame de Pompadour

of your futile namesake, the pompadour, rather
than about your own longer and more splendid and
far more abominable reign. The proceeding is not
logical: but then, as I have just pointed out to you,
Madame, the pompadour had not ever anything to
do with logic.

THE TWENTIETH LETTER:

Which Deals with a Pawnbroker

"We conceive the literal acception to be a misconstruction of the symbolical expression: apprehending a veritable history, in an emblem or piece of Christian poesy."

THE TWENTIETH LETTER:

Which Deals with a Pawnbroker

It was sixteen years ago, Messire Jurgen, since we first met; and at no later time have I regretted the hour which made us two familiar. That is well, since the outcome appears determined, that our names must be linked together for the brief while our names may hope to endure.

I regard askance this need merely in so far that, to my judgment, your history is but one chapter in the twenty chapters which compose the Biography of the Life of Manuel. I am luckier, at all events (I reflect) than are most authors whom I have heard lament that an improperly appreciative public should identify them with one particular book. Always this happened to be a book which its over-modest writer could not worship whole-heartedly, as a display of his talents in their most brilliant coruscations. But I, since the Biography is all one book (I advise myself), I am troubled by no question as to whether one book be superior to another book. My judges must debate, willy-nilly, about chapters.

In this way does logic counsel me to stay content that the tiny fraction of the public which concerns itself with such matters should select whatsoever chapter it may please them as the least inadequate chapter in my large book. Your chapter, Messire, has their suffrages. And I remark, contentedly enough, Amen!

—The more so, Messire Jurgen, for that I have long liked you as a person. This is an emotion, I pause here to observe, which during many years of tale-bearing I have not cherished invariably toward my protagonist. Indeed, now I come to think of it, you, and your father Coth, and Gerald Musgrave, and, within abrupt limits, Felix Kennaston and John Charteris—these six appear to have been the only persons about whom I have written lengthily without evoking in my own bosom something of dislike. And I wonder through what strong ob-

session any typist should have elected, throughout
the last three decades, to spend his working-hours
in the company of people whom to a degree more
or less lively he found objectionable.

*

*   *

But you, Messire, you, as a flesh-and-blood person,
I liked long before I had thought of putting you
into a book or of devising for you any adventures
. . . The boy from whom I educed my seedling notions of you, Messire Jurgen, has been dead for a
great many years: yet he too lived to be forty-and-
something, and to become commonplace in his
deeds and his thoughts, as befitted a well-to-do victim of conformity, prior to his publicly acknowledged death from even the coroner's point of view.
I prefer to remember him when he was young and
untamed and rather wonderful. I like to look back
upon our friendship, based on such candors as youth
alone may achieve or tolerate. Above all, I like to
look back upon our naïve barter of many startling
discoveries, made daily, as to mankind and religion

and biology and literature and the approved routine of seduction. And when I do look back, the way in which, at long last, I have utilized that dark and nimble and sleek-headed and impudent-eyed scapegrace would appear a little cold-blooded had experience not shown me that all of every writer's youthfulness must enter into his books, if he but lives to an age sufficiently hoary.

*

*   *

In another sense, I may declare myself to have been the benefactor of your original. There was no place for him in the South of the late 'nineties: in its unfavorable atmosphere the all-glorious and all-blundering boy whom I had known dwindled away into sedate mediocrity—and thence to a well-tended plot in the cemetery. But when once I had transferred into Poictesme the yet unconquered youngster whom I had known, throughout an ancient season of intimacy such as I interchange with few or no persons nowadays, then he thrived handsomely in a congenial clime. All his faculties found

296

employment, of a sort more or less edifying; and
he lived to the full of his nature—such, I concede
perforce, as that nature was. He became, in brief,
you, Messire Jurgen: and in this new incarnation
he stayed, as thitherto, a person over whose doings
(as one need hardly point out to you) I had remarkably little control.

It cannot well have escaped your notice, Messire,
since you also were once a poet, that it is the function of every verbal artist thus to admit others into
a world, and into a manner of living, which he admires, without admitting himself. He remains, a
lesser Moses upon a more tiny Pisgah, appreciatively
to observe, and in due course to record, the conduct
of those ephemeral tribes whom his labors have in-
ducted into the Promised Land. And to do this contents him, for a number of odd reasons which before
to-day I have set down in a number of odd places.
My point here is merely that I do not think a creator
of fiction often manufactures any character out of
the whole cloth of his fine-spun imaginings. Instead,
veracity creeps in; and old affections allure him.
Then will this lazybones begin to edit his acquaintances, or it may be himself, until the result appears
fit for its special rôle in the comedy which he fore-

Ladies and Gentlemen

plans. It was in this way, at least, that you, Messire,
got into Poictesme, just as did Guenevere and Lisa
and Anaïtis and Chloris and Steinvor and Coth, to
name but a half-dozen of your familiars.

＊

＊   ＊

But I drift into talking "literary shop" to you
whose interest in literature was limited. You liked
it, Jurgen, at its best, just as you liked all pleasure-
giving matters; yet you—you, at any event, you,
even in your flesh-and-blood youth—you had the
practical good sense to regard literature as a *hors-
d'œuvre* rather than as the main dish. You read
books with appreciation; but for no long while at
a sitting. Now and then to devise a fine jingle of
verses amused you; yet was verse-making not the
main purpose of life, you very strongly suspected,
even though at no time were you convinced as to
what might be, in mere academic point of fact, the
purpose of anything. So edifyingly temperate was
your love of letters that I may well doubt if you
would have bothered to read the history of your

298

Deals with a Pawnbroker

own life, as I have transcribed it: and that is a reflection which prompts me to become tactfully
brief.

Yet does honesty bid me report to you, Messire
Jurgen, that when the tale of your journeying was
first given to the world, in the year of grace 1919,
upon the shared feast day of St. Cosmo and St.
Damianus, it was after some deal of abridgement.
You will recall, for example, the perverse doings of
the painted boy whom you met near Gihon; that
which Merlin screened with a tapestry you must
necessarily remember no less vividly than you keep
in mind that which happened during your first visit
to Pseudopolis; nor can you very well have forgotten the obscene, lewd, lascivious and indecent ritual
of the *lithoi,* as this ceremony was performed, without any shame, by the Philistines, to commemorate
their victorious battle. You will agree with me, Messire, that such matters may not be made public
without evoking red havoc even in the proverbial
cheek of youth. All these indelicacies your biographer for this reason omitted.

At outset that availed him little, inasmuch as a
mad set of creatures, having the appearance of human adults, then read into your sword and your

299

lance and your staff such meanings as would, I think, have surprised you just as much as they did me: and for a space these creatures babbled their pruriencies. This babbling passed; this babbling mingled with the remote drivel of those paleolithic beings who, fifteen years before, had unearthed, even in the first volume I published, such wickedness "as one can parallel in nothing short of the Restoration comedies of infamous memory"; and this babbling has been well-nigh forgotten. For nothing seems more variable than is moral indignation; and of the many virtues to which well-meaning persons now and then yield, there is none other which displays its victims in lights so incredibly ludicrous by-and-by.

Through its aid did you, Messire, for some while have your undeserved reputation, as a corrupter of sophomores. I remark in consequence, with sincere pleasure, that nowadays your saga is not any longer wrested into a parable eternally ithyphallic. Instead, its general "teaching" is more generally recognized, by those partial to moralizing, as a convinced plea for monogamy, and as an exposure of the ultimate folly of any extra-matrimonial amours on the part of a married man.

Deals with a Pawnbroker

Though this doctrine be not widely popular
among the ever cocksure young, yet always it prevails by-and-by in the creed of every philosophic
male, upon whose amativeness some frank hours of
reflection and the chill of time have combined to
set limits. To this doctrine you conformed, with a
sort of half-shrugging self-derision, toward the end
of the journey which had led you back (in Kosh-
chei's uncivil phrase) to your faded termagant of a
wife . . . For middle-age had infected you through
and through, Messire, a good while before Mother
Sereda took any hand in your fortune. To lend to
a man of forty-and-something a lad's body was well
enough. Such superficial wonder-working might not
remove that ingrained ambition of the middle-aged,
about which the more humble-minded young can
know nothing.

*

*　　*

You must permit me my truism: the young seek
variety. So must the young male who is worth his
salt delight to jaunt abroad; to see and to admire

the world's strangeness; to rank the variousness and
the bright frailty of young women among the more
pleasant miracles of nature; and to seek out beauty,
and dirt, and laughter, and lust, and hard knocks,
and wonder, and sorrow, and yet other unstable fac-
tors in mankind's existence. But with age the ob-
servant come to regard such commonplaces in a
more critical vein. The human spirit turns from
these actualities to a high desire for the impossible,
in that it now craves stability. That there is in our
mortal world no stability, the middle-aged have
learned to concede, with the bluff common-sense
which rules over most middle-aged persons, like a
constitutional monarch, conditionally upon not in-
terfering with their actions. For they have learned,
also, that it is easy to produce a quite handy illu-
sion of permanence, by combining a house and a
woman—with, preferably, a cradle and a few drying
diapers in the offing. This mixture one calls
"home": and so very fortunately gullible is the nature of most graybeards that the amiable monotony
of being the legal head of a family may appear, for
the remaining part of their lives, to have been the
fixed goal of youth's seeking.

So at least you found it, Messire Jurgen, you to

Deals with a Pawnbroker

whom illusions were necessary. It is the moral of
your tale, among other morals, that you returned
home of your own fond accord—after testing a sufficient number of pleasures and palaces. Not without reason has the erudite Codman described you
as the Odysseus of Poictesme: for you journeyed
always toward your own special Penelope. And ultimately, at the winding up of so many fine adventures, you likewise shrugged, and remarked, "Well,
but I must be getting home to my wife."

In your home only, and in the discomforting
comprehension and in the loyalty and in the grim
pampering which your Lisa gave you, and in the
half-fretful tediousness of it all, might you detect
that which, at the bottom of your heart, your middle-age desired willy-nilly. After so many wander-
ings you were again safely caught in the talons of
a virtuous female: and you liked it. It was a situa-
tion as nearly permanent as any man may hope to
attain upon this side of the grave. For you were the
most thrifty of romanticists, Messire, in that you,
who had feasted with gusto at life's wide and prodi-
gal table, yet saved up the most generally acceptable
of your illusions for dessert.

About Dame Lisa one is less certain. We know

only that, like Circe—but far more like Penelope —she put forth her transforming magic. And so, not affably, not at all gently, but quite implacably, she converted the egotistic and self-reliant Jurgen into a sedately contented husband.

EXPLICIT

Palinode

Regarding the famed dead herein allied
In letters as in proverbs: ye abide
Concernless now, and heed not, in the grave,
How once ye postured—and thereafter died.

And yet, lest such epistolary flings
Rehearsing your lost lives seem flippant things
Devoid of grace and tenderness, I crave
Benignancy of you—queens, knaves, and kings.

Unite in pardon, if I utter aught
To mar your splendors; for indeed I sought,
Long and all loyally, with truth for guide
Even in my jestings, but to mar misthought
Regarding the famed dead herein allied.

Grant me forgiveness, if perchance I name
Lightly or rashly your yet-living fame
And smile upon your hurtless sins, which rest
Eternally beyond all cure or blame.

Nay, ye will pardon me—but not that wide
Zoölogy of zanies who deride
Exaltedly such fribbles as would jest
Regarding the famed dead herein allied.

www.ingramcontent.com/pod-product-compliance
Lightning Source LLC
Chambersburg PA
CBHW031201020726
47499CB00002B/444

* 9 7 8 0 8 0 9 5 3 1 2 6 4 *